BUYING and SELLING INFORMATION

What People Are Saying About
Buying and Selling Information

"It is a rare book that can transform relationships and engage all players in a sector, but *Buying and Selling Information* has that power. The Gruenberg roadmap will help librarians and sales professionals work together to successfully negotiate the future."

—Stephen Abram, MLS, Lighthouse Consulting Inc.,
and past president, SLA, CLA, OLA

"I recommend *Buying and Selling Information* as a primer for any new sales professional or developing talent and as a refresher for the more advanced professional. It's an incredibly useful reference."

—Stephen Hawthorne, executive director of Sales,
Marketing & Strategic Partnerships, Royal Society of Chemistry

"I can't think of a better person to write a book on selling in the information industry than Michael Gruenberg. He draws on his decades of experience to get to the core of what makes a salesperson tick, all couched in his own inimitable and charming style."

—Simon Beale, senior vice president and
general manager, ProQuest

"Gruenberg provides the context and framework for the rules of engagement between buyer and seller, librarian and salesperson. Following his guidance can make the buying–selling experience civilized and effective."

—Pamela Rollo, past president, SLA

"Gruenberg lays out the foundation required for establishing a successful sales representative–information professional partnership in a detailed and entertaining fashion. *Buying and Selling Information* is valuable not only to sales and information professionals but to anyone involved in the sales process in any industry."

—Michael Oakes, vice president,
Sales & Relationship Management,
Global Asset Management Solutions, Morningstar, Inc.

BUYING and SELLING INFORMATION

A Guide for
Information Professionals
and **Salespeople** to
BUILD MUTUAL SUCCESS

Michael L. Gruenberg

Information Today, Inc.
Medford, New Jersey

First printing, 2014

Buying and Selling Information: A Guide for Information Professionals and Salespeople to Build Mutual Success

Copyright © 2014 by Michael L. Gruenberg

Library of Congress Cataloging-in-Publication Data

Gruenberg, Michael L., 1946-
 Buying and selling information : a guide for information professionals and sales-people to build mutual success / Michael L. Gruenberg.
    pages cm
 Includes index.
 ISBN 978-1-57387-478-6
 1. Information services industry--Customer services. 2. Online information services industry--Customer services. 3. Libraries and publishing. 4. Libraries and electronic publishing. 5. Acquisitions (Libraries) 6. Information services--Purchasing. 7. Selling. 8. Negotiation in business. I. Title.
 HD999.I492G78 2014
 025.04068'8--dc23

                                                                 2013047034

Printed and bound in the United States of America

President and CEO: Thomas H. Hogan, Sr.
Editor-in-Chief and Publisher: John B. Bryans
Managing Editor: Amy M. Reeve
VP Graphics and Production: Norma J. Neimeister
Project Editor: Marydee Ojala
Cover Design: Lisa Conroy
Book Design: Kara Mia Jalkowski

infotoday.com

Contents

Foreword

One of the greatest professional pleasures is to share in the excitement when a colleague succeeds, and it is even greater when the colleague is a longtime friend. I greatly admire what my friend and colleague Michael Gruenberg has done with *Buying and Selling Information*.

Few subjects in our profession are more needing of attention than the relationship between those providing the products required for library clients and users, and those of us who are responsible for acquiring them.

Whether we are employed as information professionals (the term Mike and many in specialized librarianship use), specialist librarians, strategic knowledge professionals, knowledge strategists, knowledge executives, or any of the other occupations that fall somewhere among the myriad and wide-ranging lines of work relating to information and knowledge transfer, we hope to operate in trusting and practical relationships. If we do not, our clients and users are short-changed. Thanks to Mike's book, we now have expert guidance about how to work with our vendors—and how they can work with us.

Practical and actionable advice about the relationship between the information/knowledge practitioner and the vendor has long been neglected. For those of us who have been practicing for some time (I was a specialist librarian before becoming a consultant and a teacher), the solution was often catch-as-catch-can, or "learn on the job"—not the healthiest of arrangements, in terms of benefits to clients and users.

Part of the blame lays with our graduate programs, for few of them—even those teaching management to budding information and knowledge professionals—give attention to the practitioner–vendor relationship. And it is a rare occasion indeed for those moving into our profession to be given the opportunity to learn about such subjects as negotiation, contract reviews, pricing structures, sales cycles, and interactions with colleagues at trade shows (which most professionals tend to think of as conferences or, abroad, as congresses). In this book, Mike provides practical and actionable advice on these matters. From my point of view, this book should be added to the graduate curriculum for any line of work to which information and knowledge professionals aspire.

One of the great joys of Mike's book is the way he incorporates his longtime passion for popular music. It's a real treat to see the references and the connections he uses to link popular music with the varying subject matter. Through these musical anecdotes (in which his expertise is well recognized), we're given charming and truly fun links to information—and even solutions—for the issues discussed throughout the book.

The book is valuable for many reasons, some of which could be elaborated upon, but the best simply come to us as we read what Mike has written. The advice is solid ("We put ourselves in the customer's place.") and the storytelling is terrific. Embracing what we learn from this book in our working lives will open our minds to many new concepts about our and our vendors' expectations. The attention Mike gives to the value of change management and the role of leadership in our professional lives is right on target. We need to hear what he has to say.

With this book, Mike has made an important contribution to the professional literature for those who manage, what is called by many, the knowledge domain. Those of us working in the knowledge domain are well served when we read—and heed—*Buying and Selling Information.*

—Guy St. Clair

Guy St. Clair is president and knowledge services evangelist for SMR International, a New York-based consulting practice focused on change and its impact on people, organizational effectiveness, and the management of intellectual capital within the larger enterprise. He serves as special advisor to Soutron Global, the cloud-based information management and knowledge services solutions provider dedicated to implementing library transformation. At Columbia University in New York, Guy is lecturer and subject matter expert for Columbia's Master of Science in Information and Knowledge Strategy program. He is a past-president of the Special Libraries Association (SLA) and the author of *SLA's Centennial History, SLA at 100: From "Putting Knowledge to Work" to Building the Knowledge Culture* (Alexandria, VA: Special Libraries Association, 2009).

Acknowledgments

I am fortunate to continue a career that has spanned three decades and shows no signs of slowing down. I could not have survived and thrived throughout these years without an incredible group of people supporting my efforts. I would like to thank the four most influential women in my life. In the tradition of the direction, love, and support that my mother gave me so many years ago, my wife Barbara, my daughter EricaLynn, and my step daughter-in-law April have always been there for me and have always given me their candid advice, no matter how much I may have resisted some of their ideas. Thank you to my mom, Barbara, EricaLynn, and April. And thank you to my son-in-law Stephen and my stepson Iain for their advice and counsel as well.

I would also like to give a big thank you to my dear friend Irene Hoffman, whom I first met when I was a sales rep visiting her library at the University of California, Davis, far too many years ago for either one of us to recall. We've been the best of friends for over 20 years. She was the one who advised and edited my initial thoughts and organized the writings of this book. Her counsel has been invaluable, and I cherish our friendship.

On a professional level, there are colleagues who need to be acknowledged. Not a day goes by in my business career when I don't think about my late dear friend Steve Goldspiel and the profound influence he has had on my life. He was my boss, friend, and confidant. We shared secrets and strategies for sales and life, and all the while had fun building a company. His unorthodox style and panache have guided me in so many ways, both professionally and personally. I can't thank him enough for bringing me into this magical world of sales.

My father's wisdom and guidance are still the cornerstone of my daily activities, and only two other people on this planet have taught me as much about life as he did: Phil Hixon and Bob Snyder. They owned Disclosure and taught me how to be successful in business. They guided me, and, under their direction, their employees turned a sleepy $1.7M company into a $100M powerhouse of a company. I was blessed to climb the corporate ladder from sales rep to global vice president of sales during their tenure. My great joy was being able to work once again for Bob at CSA and for his son Andy at ProQuest later in my career.

I would like to thank all the salespeople I had the pleasure to know and manage over these 30+ years. I learned so much from you guys. I especially want to thank Chris Arthur, whose charm and hard work were fundamental to our success as a sales group. She and I worked together for 18 years, and every day with her was a pleasure.

I'd also like to thank the many information professionals who welcomed me into their libraries, listened to my stories, and politely laughed at my jokes, and whose friendships I still treasure to this day.

When the publisher of the book told me that he had assigned Marydee Ojala to be the editor of *Buying and Selling Information*, I was both relieved and honored. I was relieved because Marydee and I have been friends for virtually all of the years that I have been in the business of selling information. If anyone knows me, she does. I am honored because she is one of those people in our business who truly understands the information industry. Her insights, frank appraisals, and knowledge of libraries have guided me in writing the book. I would also like to extend my heartfelt thanks to Amy Reeve, Managing Editor, Books Division, at Information Today, Inc. I will always be grateful for her incredible job of organizing my random thoughts into a cohesive book.

I met Matt Dunie about 25 years ago when I spoke at an industry seminar. He was new to his job at that time, and he came up to me after the presentation and was very kind in his comments about the subject matter I had discussed. About 20 years later, when he was president at CSA, I went to work for him. Since then, he and I have collaborated on a number of projects. A big thank you to Matt, my friend and business colleague.

Finally, this book could not even have been thought about or written without my mentor and dear friend Jay Shelov. Jay has been the rock of my career. His knowledge and encouragement have guided me through the best of times and even the bleakest of times. I am truly blessed to have had him, his wife, and his daughter in my life. I think of all of them often with great fondness.

Preface

On January 3, 1977, I began my first job as a salesperson. Given that my previous work experience was as a teacher and licensed principal in the New York City school system, along with part-time work as a musician, I wondered what the odds were that my new job in sales would last more than a year.

Looking back, I'd say that even if the odds were against me, I made the right bet, as I have functioned and thrived as a senior sales executive for more than 35 years in the information industry. In that time, I have successfully sold information products to libraries all over the world. Moreover, as vice president of sales for a number of organizations, I have supervised and trained a significant number of salespeople in how to successfully manage their relationships with their library prospects/customers. By understanding the concept of mutual cooperation, I have encouraged sales reps and information professionals to work together to create a mutually beneficial partnership.

Too often salespeople return from meetings and report to their manager that they are hoping for an order, when in fact neither the rep nor the customer firmly grasped the reason for the meeting in the first place. How could anyone expect to write business if the rep and client are not even on the same page?

In 2012, I wrote an article for the March/April issue of *Information Outlook*, a magazine published by the Special Libraries Association, describing how the salesperson and the information professional each needed to prepare for the sales meeting. Since then, that article has been widely read, translated into Japanese, and well received by salespeople and librarians alike.

I decided to expand on the article and write a book on how a better understanding of the buying and selling process benefits both the information professional and the salesperson. When both parties are better prepared for a sales meeting, they achieve a higher level of communication and better results.

For the information professional, whether just graduated from library school or on the job for decades, this book is a critical guide to navigating a process that can, at times, be overwhelming. How does a representative of the library come though the sales process successfully? Perhaps it is by negotiating a better price for the goods and services being sold. Perhaps it is by remembering that the vendor does not have the ability to sell the library something not needed or wanted. Or perhaps a successful negotiation means earning recognition as an employee of stature amongst colleagues.

It's all about equal footing, momentum, and success. The information professional who understands and uses the knowledge presented here will be much better prepared and, as such, more successful in dealing with salespeople.

Too often over the years, I met with librarians who proceeded to tell me that my product was great but that they couldn't possibly afford to buy it. There is no reason for a librarian to ask a salesperson to visit the library and present a product if, in fact, there is no chance of the product being bought. On the other hand, if the salesperson is made aware that the visit is strictly for exploratory reasons and money for purchase may be available at a later date, then his time is not wasted. However, more often than not, I found out that the "no money" line was more defense mechanism than actuality.

Still, how much time would have been saved if the librarian had embraced the sales process and worked with the sales rep to figure out a way to make a purchase happen? If the product presented is appropriate for the patrons of the library, and if the product is priced reasonably, then the rep and the info pro need to work together to make the sale happen. This book encourages that cooperation.

While a person must go to graduate school to get an MLIS degree to be employed as a librarian, there are no such requirements for someone to become a salesperson. Truly, anyone can become a salesperson. As a result, there are many salespeople who, in actuality, are better suited for another line of employment. We've all encountered these people at a department store, fast-food restaurant, or boutique: Their body language, lack of people skills, and demeanor cry out that they would rather be anywhere else than in that store serving the public.

A successful sales rep is one who knows his product, likes interacting with people, and wants his customers to be satisfied. In dealing with information professionals—by and large, a pleasant group—the sales rep has an opportunity to be a champion by bringing to the library's attention a product or service that will be of benefit to the users of the library and the organization. This book is designed to help any sales rep gain a better understanding of the process an information professional must cope with internally to select and purchase information products.

When each understands the other's roles and responsibilities, the sale rep becomes more efficient and the librarian becomes a more informed consumer. This book helps both librarians and salespeople to outthink and outperform their colleagues. It's a book about mutual benefit.

Writing this book is the culmination of a dream that started after a sales meeting at a library many years ago, when it occurred to me that I needed to write a book about everything I was experiencing while working through the sales process. If you gain one fact though the reading of this book that makes you better in your professional and maybe even your personal life, then I have fulfilled that dream.

Introduction

My career in the information industry began with a phone call to a friend:

> "Hi Steve, this is Mike Gruenberg. It's been a while since we last spoke."
>
> "Hi Mike, it's great to hear from you again. How are you doing? It's been at least 2 years since I last saw you," he said in a welcoming manner. "So, what's going on in your life?"

What's going on in my life? I asked myself. *Where should I start?* And with those words, without my knowing it, the very early seeds of this book began to take root.

I first met Steve Goldspiel when we taught school together in Williamsburg, Brooklyn. After getting married, I earned my masters in educational administration and supervision, which allowed me to become permanently certified as a principal in the New York State School system.

Steve, on the other hand, went from teaching to working in an insurance and brokerage business for a few years. That didn't work out, so he got a job as a salesman. He explained to me on the phone that the product he was selling was financial information filed by public companies at the U.S. Securities and Exchange Commission. The information was contained in books and microfiche, and it was sold to librarians at financial institutions.

I told Steve that literally on the same day I received my principal's certification, I was informed that, due to the seriousness of the New York City budget crisis, my job had been eliminated. Since that fateful day, I had endured a series of unfulfilling positions as a substitute teacher at various schools in Brooklyn and Queens.

Steve was one of those people who always had a lot of creative ideas and seemingly knew many people across a variety of industries. I explained to him that I had recently gotten married and my wife and I wanted to start a family, but not having a permanent job was making it difficult to plan ahead.

"Do you have any advice as to my next move in finding a job? Do you know anyone I could call to help me?" I asked him.

Without hesitation, he strongly suggested that I become a salesperson. He had just been promoted to New York regional sales manager for his company, and there was an opening in that office for a salesperson.

And from that moment, everything changed in my life:

> "You think I can be a salesperson?" I said incredulously.
>
> "You are a natural salesperson," he replied.
>
> "But, Steve, I'm not sure that I want to be a salesperson, and I don't even know the first thing about how to sell!" I stated emphatically.
>
> "Yes, you do know how to sell," Steve replied. "I think you can be very successful as a salesperson, and I am expecting you to meet me at my office on Monday at 11 AM for an interview. If you still really hate the idea after I explain the opportunity to you, then at the very least, we'll have lunch together," he said.

As I hung up the phone, I had no inkling as to what that appointment would mean for me in relation to the rest of my life. I showed up at his office, interviewed for the job, and enjoyed a visit with my old friend. He had this incredible quality of making you feel that you were the most important person in the room. Even though I hadn't seen or spoken to him for at least 2 years, it was as though we had been together just the day before.

By the end of lunch, I was enthused, confused, and overwhelmed with the possibilities of what I might be able to accomplish as a salesperson. On January 3, 1977, I became a full-fledged salesman for a company called Disclosure. I worked many years for Steve, who later became the president of the company. This man, my friend and mentor, guided my professional development from salesperson to vice president of sales. I spent 20 years at Disclosure, working with the most talented and dedicated staff of professionals. It was a privilege to work there.

What I thought was going to be a 6-month, stop-gap interlude, leading me back to a teaching appointment, turned into a lifetime career in sales. It's a job that has taken me to libraries, universities, and speaking engagements all over the world. It has afforded me a lifestyle and income that I could never have imagined or duplicated as a teacher. My time spent in sales and sales management have thus far given me 35 years of cherished experiences and promises an even brighter outlook for the future.

This book is meant to guide salespeople and information professionals through the process of successfully buying and selling information. This is not just another "rules of the game" book written by someone who never did it: It is based on the real-life stories, situations, and experiences that I coped with, analyzed, and figured out. It explains how these lessons helped build my career and earn the trust of my customers.

A word about the terminology used in the book: A person who sells a product or service to the library is referred to here as the *salesperson*, *sales rep*, or *rep*. All these terms refer to the person who has products/services/databases to sell. Similarly, the person who buys the products/services/databases is referred to in the book as an *information professional*, *info pro*, or *librarian*.

In the chapters that follow, you will discover how the participants in the process of buying and selling data can work together—not as adversaries, but as a team. I will cover how each individual—information professional or salesperson—can effectively prepare for a successful sales meeting, and what both parties should do both during and after the meeting to make it relevant and valuable to both (e.g., what is appropriate in terms of follow-up, and how you can negotiate to create a win–win situation). There is information on tools, tactics, and advice—all drawn from my own personal experiences.

By understanding what the salesperson is trying to accomplish and the steps he is taking to achieve that goal, information professionals will know what to be aware of, and how to prepare for a sales meeting and make the meeting and follow-up productive for both parties. Furthermore, the information professional can ask, What lessons have I learned from the salesperson who just visited me? How can I apply that knowledge to improve my dealings with the departments and people within my library?

To me, writing music and building business relationships share some remarkable similarities. Although it's been reported that The Rolling Stones' Keith Richards and Mick Jagger composed "Satisfaction" in 20 minutes in the middle of the night, writing a song is typically a longer process. The composer often initially experiments with various themes and melodies before attempting to match lyrics to the notes. It's a process that can take as little as a few hours or as long as a few years. The composer and/or lyricist will take as much time as is necessary to get it right.

Much like writing a song, building a successful business relationship can take many years of trial and error. Sometimes sales reps and their customers have differences of opinion. That doesn't mean one is right and the other is wrong. It just means that in order to successfully complete their business dealings, each one has to work with diligence to understand the goals and objectives of the other. Salespeople will do their best to overcome objections while information professionals will deliberate over the relative worth of the product being presented. A strong business relationship is the result of many years of working together.

Because crafting a song and building a business relationship are so similar, I have chosen to begin each chapter of *Buying and Selling Information* with a brief mention of a song that, for me, reflects the topic to be discussed. I hope the songs that I have chosen evoke pleasant memories for you.

Finally, throughout the book, I feature many personal stories. They are a compilation of my varied experiences and the myriad people I have had the pleasure of meeting. Every story is based on actual events.

THE INFO PRO–SALESPERSON RELATIONSHIP

 "Help, I need somebody. Help, not just anybody," sang The Beatles in "Help" (written by John Lennon and Paul McCartney). We may not be trying to escape bad guys, as John, Paul, George, and Ringo were in the film of the same name, but we all need help in some way when buying and selling information.

An agreement is reached, a relationship is developed, and a sale is made. It's the result of two or more people working together to achieve a mutually acceptable objective. A vendor has an electronic resource product to sell and the library has a need for that data. In this section of the book, I will examine how the information professional and the sales rep begin the journey of buying and selling data. How do they establish mutual trust and respect? When both parties are working cooperatively, both derive benefit.

Building the buyer–seller relationship includes many factors, including the concept of "reading the room." The way in which an office is arranged tells a great deal about a person. As a sales rep or info pro, we all go to someone else's office to conduct business affairs. Learning to take note of the room and using that knowledge for the meeting is a skill set that can help you understand the person with whom you are dealing.

The art of communication is also critical in relationship building—more specifically, how to choose the right words, communicate effectively, and establish bonds. Many a motivational speaker has said, "You never get a second chance to make a first impression." While that is certainly true, establishing bonds and communicating is an ongoing process, especially in the buying and selling process, because the time from initial contact to final sale can take months, even years. Therefore, it is critical for everyone's success that both parties consistently communicate effectively with one another.

In addition to these topics, this section will examine how to make trade shows work more effectively for buyer and seller, when and how to be persistent, and how, when each party does more than his or her share, a successful sale is the result.

People Do Business With People, *Not* With Companies

 In the Broadway musical *Funny Girl*, Barbra Streisand sang, "People who need people are the luckiest people in the world" (written by Jule Styne and Bob Merrill). We not only need other people in both our personal and business lives, but we also need to know more about the people we are attempting to do business with.

"People do business with people, not with companies" is perhaps the single most appropriate phrase to describe how business should be conducted. Because the bottom line is that it takes people to make a deal, it takes people to negotiate with one another, and it takes people to conclude the deal. When I negotiate with Dan from XYZ Corporation, I am sitting across the table from Dan and he is my window into the workings of the company he represents. If Dan is smart, I inevitably think that XYZ Corp. hires bright people. If he's less than intelligent, my view of that company is greatly diminished.

Librarians and salespeople, you are the representatives of your respective organizations. How you come across to the other person speaks volumes about you and the entity you represent. Throughout this book, I will give you guidelines not only on how to make a great first impression but also on how to carry that through to the final deal and for as long as the two of you are conducting business together.

My father arrived in this country in 1939. He was close to 40 years old at that time and needed to make a living as quickly as possible, and the surest way to do that was to become a salesperson. He struggled early on, learned the nuances of the language, and familiarized himself with American business practices, all of which led to a new career late in life for him. He achieved some degree of success and always told me that the key to anyone's success in sales is to establish a relationship with the customer. He often said, "Mike, I don't care if you're selling Cadillacs or pencils; the successful sales rep is successful because he knows his customers and his customers like and trust him."

We not only need people in our personal and business lives; we need to know more *about* them. This chapter will talk about how the information professional and the sales rep can get to know one another and thus pave the way to a successful relationship for both.

Reading the Room

It takes more than one meeting to develop a relationship between a salesperson and a potential customer. Trust is developed over a period of time as both parties get to know one another. Ultimately, people learning from one another is what lays the groundwork for a successful relationship.

Many salespeople get so preoccupied with their presentation, or the importance of the meeting, or even whatever personal issues they are coping with, that they forget to *read the room*. When this happens, they miss a golden opportunity to get to know their intended customer a little better.

For a salesperson, reading the room simply means looking around and being aware of what the customer is looking at every day. By taking note of the items displayed, perceptive sales reps will better understand with whom they are dealing. In doing so, they get to know the customer even before any words have been exchanged.

Let's consider the following example. Bill is a salesperson and has just gotten an appointment with a prospect he has been trying to see for the last year; let's call her Judy. He has seen Judy at trade shows, has done extensive research on her needs, and has determined that the new Whiz Bang database recently developed by his company makes perfect sense for the art collection in Judy's library. He believes this is an opportune time to meet with Judy because his company is offering a significant discount to new customers who commit to purchase the Whiz Bang database within the next 60 days.

At his weekly one-on-one meeting with his sales manager, Bill finds out that he can earn a double commission on every sale of the new Whiz Bang database if he can close the order by the end of the following month.

How lucky am I? Bill thinks to himself. *I've got an appointment with a great prospect I've been chasing for months, I have the product she needs, I know her library is well-funded for this subject matter, and when I sell Whiz Bang to her, I'll get a fat commission and a happy customer!*

Bill certainly has the incentive to succeed both professionally and personally, since he has been under quota for most of the year and has been getting pressure from his boss to perform at a higher level. A sale here would solve a host of problems, not the least of which is keeping his job.

Following up on his research, Bill sends Judy an agenda the week before the meeting, and, much to his delight, she immediately responds by sending back a note thanking him and adding two more items for discussion at the meeting.

The big day arrives, and Bill shows up armed with a PowerPoint presentation as well as some research he has done in advance. He is so focused on his presentation that he forgets to look around the room. Judy's office is filled with pictures of her family. On her desk is a photo of Judy and her significant other along with two young children whitewater rafting. Hanging directly above her desk is a large framed picture of the family at a carousel. Finally, there is poster board with children's handprints in paint taped on the wall saying "Love You Mommy." Unfortunately for Bill, he fails to notice any of the signs around the room and launches immediately into his presentation.

Bill has committed one of the great sins of omission by not tailoring his presentation to the person with whom he is speaking. Clearly, Judy loves her family. Taking notice of the photos and expressing interest in them would have invited Judy into the conversation and made it clear that her input and thoughts are important for good communication. An exchange of thoughts, ideas, and preferences between parties is necessary in any good relationship, and by engaging in light conversation prior to getting into the topics of the meeting, both parties may become more comfortable with one another.

Bill should have looked around the room and picked up an understanding of what type of person Judy is. Judy gave Bill all the opening signs he needed, had he just used his eyes.

When reading the room, all salespeople need to remember that most of us are guided by one of four basic principles:

1. **Recognition:** You can assume a person thrives on recognition if he posts awards on his wall; that person is proud of his accomplishments and wants you to know it. People who crave recognition usually have large egos and need to be spoken to in a certain manner: "So, Jim, that's a pretty impressive award you have there. How did you manage to achieve such an honor?"

2. **Love:** Many pictures of family and friends on someone's desk indicate that love is very important to them. A good way to begin a conversation with this person might be: "Great picture of you and the kids. Was that taken at Yellowstone Park? My family went there a few years ago and had a great time."

3. **Money:** A person with nicely framed artwork on her walls or high-end furniture in her office takes pride in

being able to afford the finer things. The best way to begin this meeting may be to say: "What a beautiful leather chair."

4. **Self-preservation:** A person who is most concerned with self-preservation is just trying to get through the day. There may be papers in no particular order all over his desk or files in stacks in various corners of the office. The person who obviously lacks organization may require extra attention. At the end of the meeting, perhaps close by saying: "I'll be sure to follow up with a summary of our meeting and a reminder of our next appointment."

Most of the time, people will tell you without words who they are just by what is found in their work space. A person with plush toys scattered about is very different from a person with expensive artwork. A person who has pictures of himself posing with famous people is different from a person who proudly displays artwork by his children. A librarian's office adorned with an autographed photo of a politician or a plaque proclaiming some important achievement can also reveal quite a bit.

At the very least, it's an opening for a conversation that will let the parties get to know each other better before the business discussion begins. And after all, in this competitive world, isn't it wise to know as much as possible about the person you are hoping to do business with? The salesperson cannot even begin to think about making the sale until he gets to know the person sitting on the other side of the desk, and the info pro cannot hope to get the right product without letting the sales rep know the library's precise needs.

I recently conducted training for a client's sales staff where I spoke about reading the room. One of the reps asked if I had looked around their offices before my presentation so I could learn a little about the participants. In fact, I had studied one particular office and noticed it was quite stark—no photos of family or friends on the wall or on the desk. The only prominent item was a special reserve bottle of Jameson Irish Whiskey. I surmised that the individual occupying this office was either proud of his Irish heritage or willing to pay top dollar for his liquor, if not both.

Information professionals who are reluctant to reveal their personal tastes and values to salespeople may be better served holding their meetings in a conference room or some other neutral meeting space within the library. However, a person's "inner sanctum" reveals a nonbusiness side, and an astute rep can build on this sort of information. A rep who carries on a more personal conversation also tells the info pro a lot about how the rep will handle the business needs of the library.

After all, people really don't do business with companies; they do business with other people. If both parties can relate to one another on a business *and* personal level, they have a better than average chance of reaching their individual goals.

Getting to Know Each Other

In the interest of establishing a strong salesperson–customer relationship, it behooves the sales rep and the information professional to learn as much as they can about each other. For the salesperson, knowing the customer is the first step in building success; for the librarian, knowing the company he may soon rely on as an information provider is equally important.

Just a note on internet reconnaissance before continuing: Thanks largely to the web and social media, there are more ways than ever before for the parties to learn about one another, and I suggest using these resources in the sections that follow. But while the internet is a treasure trove of information, the information on websites and social networks should be used with care. I once worked for a firm that was acquired by another company, and naturally, my colleagues and I were quite interested in the direction and policies of the new ownership group. We learned that some employees of the company that acquired us had established a blog about the company's management team. Many of their postings were less than complimentary, and while we read the blog with a grain of salt, some of the comments did make us wonder.

Nevertheless, the blog entries gave us a general idea of what we might expect and allowed us to be more prepared when the new management came to town to meet their new employees. Similarly, information on a blog may be useful to a salesperson or info pro when preparing for that initial sales meeting, but it is important to consider the source and be skeptical.

Getting to Know the Vendor and the Salesperson

Libraries represent a lucrative market for information providers, and, as a result, the librarian holds an enormous amount of leverage when dealing with the many data providers that call every day. According to Outsell's 2010 Information Industry Market Size Share & Forecast Report, "Excluding news and yellow pages and directories, the $368.5 billion information industry started to rebound in 2010 with the remaining segments predicted to post 4.8 percent combined growth in 2010." Given the fact that currently there is a finite number of libraries being serviced by a relatively small group of vendors, information professionals should expect to be actively courted for their business by competing vendors. Odds are that a vendor selling a business database will most certainly have a competitor offering a similar product. It's up to the info pro to do her homework and select a vendor that has the most appropriate product at the most appropriate price. In this multibillion dollar business environment, the enlightened vendor is the one only too glad to offer libraries incentives so that the business comes its way and does not go to a competitor. It's up to the info pro to examine all aspects of the product presented, demand the best possible terms, and extol the vendor that meets the library's needs and budget.

Knowing the information vendor is the first step in finding success as a customer. Prior to any substantive meeting with a salesperson, the information professional must research the company being represented. Websites, blogs, news articles, and press releases can all provide background on the good, the bad, and the ugly of the firm that wants your business. Information Today, Inc.'s NewsBreaks (newsbreaks.infotoday. com) and Outsell, Inc.'s Information Industry Headlines (outsellinc.com/our_industry/headlines) offer background on information companies in general, while Scope e-Knowledge Center's Knowledgespeak newsletter (delivered daily by email) concentrates on scientific and medical resources and companies.

Additionally, I have always found that the global collegial network of librarians and information professionals is a great source of information about vendors. Use that network, inquire of friends and colleagues, and acquire a working knowledge of the most applicable products in relation to the library's resources when considering what to buy and from whom. It also can't hurt to ask a potential vendor for the names of current customers who can serve as references. Contacting these individuals will be useful and sometimes even eye-opening, as librarians and other information professionals tend to give honest opinions to their peers.

Other questions the information professional will want answered regarding the vendor include the following:

- How does the rep's company stack up against its competition?

- What is the financial health of the vendor?

- What is the vendor's longevity? Are they in it for the long haul? Is the company a candidate to be acquired in the near future and, if so, how would that effect the library's database subscriptions?

- What products from this company are the best fit for the library's collection?

- Does the company in general have a good or bad reputation in the industry?

- What type of technical support can the library expect?

- Does the company have a strong track record of keeping the promises made to customers about its technology?

- Is training available? If so, how frequently and by whom (by staff with MLS degrees)?

- Does the company have a purchasing process that is acceptable to the library? Will the library's purchasing procedures prove too difficult for the company to follow?

- Does the rep have more than adequate knowledge about the products that will be presented? Can the salesperson describe and demo the product effectively *without* a PowerPoint presentation?

Getting to Know the Information Professional

I have worked in the information industry for over three decades. In that time, I have called on libraries all over the world and sold a multitude of information products. While I never owned a database producing company, I know it's a good business to be in. Salespeople provide libraries with valuable data for which libraries are willing to pay. But information professionals recognize that it's a very competitive business; if a salesperson is not earning an information professional's trust and respect, odds are that she will begin to explore the other available options.

Much like the library customer, a sales rep needs to actively prepare for all substantive sales meetings. Conducting research on the library to be visited is an essential part of that preparation. Library websites are chock full of valuable facts about the organization. Many feature a message written by the library director right on the homepage. By knowing the vision of the director, a salesperson can tailor the presentation to include products that are in keeping with the institution's objectives.

Salespeople should read websites, blogs, news articles, and press releases to gain additional background. At the very least, when the rep is able to demonstrate an understanding of the library's goals and objectives, the librarian will know he has gone through a process of research that the competition may or may not match. The salesperson's observations and attention to detail will impress the individual on the other side of the desk.

For the sales rep, knowing the customer is a very involved process. Whether it's a company, university, public library, association, or government agency, significant pieces of information need to be obtained and connected in order for the rep to understand the workings of the organization he's calling upon. Without a thorough grasp and appreciation of the customer's world, the rep will not be able to provide the most successful solutions to her needs.

The salesperson can start to learn about the customer by getting answers to the following questions:

- Does the library value long-term relationships with vendors?

- Does the institution have a track record of meeting its financial commitments? Is it in sound fiscal health?

- When does the customer intend to complete the purchase? Are they looking to some future date or ready to commit now? If they are looking to the future, what does that represent in terms of real time? (Many a rep has failed to ask the following pivotal question. "If I give you the greatest sales presentation you've ever seen, how long will it take for a commitment to be made to buy the product?")

- What similar products are already being used successfully at peer libraries or perhaps already by the prospective customer?

Communicating Effectively and Creating Bonds

I have always maintained that the first step in a mutually beneficial relationship is establishing the ability to communicate effectively. Whether it's a business or personal connection, calling, seeing, and meeting with the other person allows us to eliminate any doubts regarding purpose.

By the same token, I don't believe you can really "know" another person without some form of ongoing communication. A continuing dialogue over time allows us to form deeper levels of understanding and appreciation for one another's needs and goals.

When I first began selling to academic libraries, I was the only rep for the entire country to cover that market. Over the years, as the business increased, my travel schedule needed more planning. Through careful time management, I was able to schedule a good mix of new business appointments and renewal calls. By virtue of the academic market I served, most of my calls were not in major metropolitan city centers; while commercial market sales reps were going to Chicago, San Francisco, and Boston, I was traveling to places like Lubbock (TX), Hanover (NH), and Lawrenceville (NJ).

Many times when I showed up at a relatively out-of-the-way location, the librarian would tell me that most of the reps she'd dealt with previously had conducted their business over the phone. To me, it always was—and still is—worth the trip to meet face-to-face with a client. Phone conversations and WebEx, SKYPE, FaceTime, and so on are great, but they will never replace personal, face-to-face contact.

I'm willing to bet that a significant reason an information professional might prefer one vendor over another is the number of visits its reps have made to the library. Visiting a customer's library on a regular basis shows an interest on the part of the company and its rep, creates a bond between the librarian and the rep, and paves the way for a productive long-term relationship.

I once attended a state library association meeting in a western state not often visited by sales reps. At the last minute, the sales rep who covered that state called to say he could not be there. Since the company considered the state library to be a key prospect, I was pressed into service as the lone company attendee, travelling from the east coast out to the west.

Much to my surprise, our competition sent a delegation of three people to this small conference. Not only was the local rep there, but a VP and a customer support person were there too. Three months later, we lost out on a request for proposal (RFP) in that state to the competition. Our competitors knew that a strong show of support to the customer would cement a possible relationship on the RFP bid.

Not every call a salesperson makes to a library involves a product pitch, nor should it. Part of what creates a strong bond between the librarian and the sales rep is follow-up communication at regular intervals. That communication can take the form of a phone call or an in-person visit. If a rep is visiting another account in the customer's area, a brief visit just to say hello makes sense and is a great way to build the relationship.

Of course, for a salesperson to drop in to say hello to the customer without appearing rude, the two parties must have already established a comfortable relationship that allows for this. It's even more unacceptable if the sales rep just shows up at the librarian's door expecting to have a substantive meeting. As a rule, the sales rep should always inform the customer of the intent to visit at a specific time and date. The information professional needs to discourage sales reps from dropping in for any purpose and instead encourage advance notice of any type of meeting. A conversation I've had many times over the years goes something like this:

> "Hi, Ed. I'm literally around the corner from you and would love to drop by to say a quick hello. Are you free at 10?"
>
> "Sure, come on by, Mike, but I only have a few minutes."
>
> "That's fine, Ed, I have an appointment at 10:45. I'm at a coffee shop. Can I get you a cup of coffee and a bagel?"

The purpose of this type of visit is to say hello and see how things are going. Casual visits like this build strong relationships that help both parties when the more formal appointments eventually take place.

Another great way for an information professional and sales rep to create a closer bond is to plan ahead to get together at trade shows. Many companies hold receptions and similar customer-oriented events at these shows, and although the marketing department is tasked with sending out the invitations, it's up to each rep to make sure all his clients are on the list. These types of receptions provide a relaxed atmosphere conducive to socializing.

I'd like to share two examples of how effective communication between customers and sales reps has made all the difference for me in my career. The first example involves someone I worked with more than 20 years ago—a librarian at a major investment firm that was among my accounts at the time. I recently received a communication from her through LinkedIn congratulating me on establishing my consulting company. Reading her message brought back the memory of a relationship that had taken many years to develop.

At our first meeting all those years ago, she seemed reluctant to fully participate; in fact, I'd describe her demeanor as stand-offish. Many of the database products we discussed, and which

I subsequently recommended for purchase, were met with skepticism. Eventually the investment firm became a customer, but the initial deal took years to close.

I was always keenly aware of her attitude and, as a result, tried to do whatever I could, whenever I could, to create a positive environment for us to do business together. I made it a point to try and visit with her whenever I was in town, and many of those calls were just to say hello or share a cup of coffee. When our conversations turned to matters other than business—our latest vacations or what our families were up to, for instance—it was almost as though I was speaking with a different person. She became more open and animated, and we clearly enjoyed those conversations more than the business ones. She had a great personality and a terrific sense of humor, which I would not have known from our business discussions.

I can't put my finger on the moment when our business relationship turned around, but there came a time when she was noticeably more relaxed during our meetings. As we got to know one another, I encouraged her to spend more time with salespeople:

> "Who better than a salesperson to update you on the latest trends and products?" I said. "If the rep is *not* prepared and knowledgeable about these things, you'll know it immediately. And guess what? You can either counsel him to be more prepared the next time or ask the company to send someone better informed. Either way," I pointed out, "you are in control of the situation."

This point bears reiterating: If the salesperson is not doing his job satisfactorily in the opinion of the information professional, the information professional has every right to request a different rep be assigned to the account. It happens, more often than most reps would like to believe.

Getting back to my client, when I was promoted to VP of sales at my company I called her to let her know that, due to my new position, I would not be able to handle the account on a day-to-day basis, but that given how important she was to me as a customer and colleague, I intended to remain very much in the picture. I explained that even with a new rep servicing her account, I planned to check in with her from time to time.

Of course, I accompanied the new sales rep on his first meeting with her. Her old skepticism was present that day, but, among the three of us, we found common ground, and the meeting concluded successfully. A few days later, she called to thank me for the personal introduction to her new rep.

So here we are, after more than 20 years, still communicating. Her recent LinkedIn email was not only to congratulate me on establishing my consulting firm but also to remind me of the advice I gave her so many years ago: that engaging with salespeople on a regular basis could help her become more successful in her own work. She described it as the best business advice she had ever given.

The second example I want to share involves another relationship I developed a long time ago and that came back to me in the last position I worked in before starting my consulting practice. In that role, I worked with the company's "Most Valuable Accounts," or MVAs.

To qualify as an MVA, a customer had to meet one or more of three criteria:

1. Represent a specific dollar threshold of sales revenue

2. Have the potential to reach a specific dollar threshold of sales revenue

3. Represent an account that was in need of special attention or handling for future sales or renewals

Included on the list of possible MVA candidates at the time was a library director from a major Midwestern university whom

I knew quite well. I had been her sales rep when she was working at another prestigious university in the east, where I followed her rise to dean of the library school and library director. However, after many years, I had lost touch with her.

I sent her a "Remember Me?" email to reconnect and to let her know about my new role as director of the MVA program. To my delight, she responded immediately and we promised to get together as soon as possible.

In discussing this exchange with the regional sales manager, I learned that he had been working with this university for many years and that, while its total spending with our company was already considerable, he was proposing a more inclusive database subscription package that, if accepted, would make them one of our largest accounts.

Given the importance of the university both as an MVA and major account, I suggested to the regional sales manager that we make a trip together to ensure we were doing everything we could to satisfy the customer on as many levels as possible. He agreed and worked up a full-day schedule of meetings for us at the university.

Coming in the night before our meeting, I arranged to have dinner with my old acquaintance. Though it had been years since we'd communicated, it was as if no time had passed at all. We talked about our careers and our families, and enjoyed a most pleasant evening.

The following day, the regional manager and I conducted a series of meetings at the university with various members of the library staff. Our last meeting of the day was with my friend to review and debrief the discussions with her staff.

We had a productive dinner meeting with her, and, as it came to an end, she turned to my colleague and said, "When I was a young librarian, it was Mike who taught me how to communicate with salespeople, and I'll always be grateful for that advice and direction." Needless to say, it was a great compliment, and it also served to reinforce what I have been saying to information professionals all these many years.

As a postscript to this story, the regional sales manager's team subsequently closed a seven-figure deal with the university, making it the largest order from that region in the history of the company.

These two examples demonstrate the power of communication between customers and sales reps, and how business relationships form, evolve, and succeed over time through communication.

KNOWLEDGE POINTS

- People do business with people; people do *not* do business with companies.

- By getting to know their prospects, sales reps are able to understand more about whom they are meeting with, their needs, and their goals.

- An astute salesperson will look around the customer's office upon arrival and take note of what is on display. Those items will tell quite a bit about the person.

- The sales rep and customer should take time to get to know each other personally, since this personal relationship will help them develop a more thorough professional relationship. If the rep is paying attention to personal details before the sale, the customer may very well assume that the rep will also continue to pay attention after the sale is completed.

- The sales rep needs to earn the trust of the information professional and the right to serve as the primary contact between the library and the company.

- Communication is the key to success and can take the form of both formal and informal outreach.

CHAPTER

It Takes Two

"It takes two" sang Marvin Gaye and Kim Weston in the hit song of the same name (written by Sylvia Moy and William Stevenson). It's true that one person cannot make a deal— it does, in fact, take two. And one person cannot negotiate with himself—again, it takes two.

I strongly believe that salespeople and librarians are in the same business: helping people. The sales meeting is a consultative process enhanced by a set of business guidelines on both sides so that the meeting covers all the pertinent facts that need to be reviewed and answered. An orderly process will help both the information professional and sales rep find the best solution. Negotiation skills should not be limited to the sales side of the relationship; information professionals need to be just as proficient as sales reps when it comes to negotiation. Information professionals can learn from their sales reps, and vice versa.

Guidelines for the Salesperson and the Vendor

The overall mantra of the book is, "Selling is helping people make decisions that are good for them." Good sales representatives understand that their role is to help their customers. They clearly understand that there is more than one vendor that any customer in any industry can go to and buy virtually the same product. Librarians have many choices as to which database products they can buy, what companies they prefer to buy them from, and which salespeople they choose to work with.

Sales success is rented; it's not self-perpetuating. Smart reps know they need to earn their customers' trust and respect every day. That atmosphere of trust and mutual respect becomes the cornerstone of the relationship. When customers are taken for granted, they go away. Unless the situation is corrected, shortly thereafter, the business goes away and, in the end, the rep goes away.

To determine the appropriate products to present and sell, a salesperson needs to understand the needs of the library. Once the need is discovered, then and only then can the salesperson even begin to consider what recommendations to make to the information professional.

The truly successful sales professional follows these guidelines:

1. **Know yourself:** That's right, what kind of sales rep are you? Do you have the stamina and drive to conduct a full day of appointments? A good salesperson looks to fill the day with qualified appointments. Is this "just a job" or a career? Because if it's only a job, your longevity may be tenuous.

2. **Set goals:** There are different types of goals: personal, professional, and financial. Some people have 30-day goals; some have 6-month goals; and others take a long view of the entire year. A career goal may be to earn a promotion to manager or director. A personal goal may be to make enough money at your day job to support a growing family. No matter what your goals are, they need to be written down, acknowledged, reviewed constantly, and revised on a regular basis.

3. **Be truthful:** As my longtime mentor said to me, "Never lie, cheat, steal, or deceive." Be able to look yourself in the mirror and inwardly know that you have given the best possible service to every one of your customers each and every day.

The vendor should also have a set of guidelines that must be understood and followed by every employee who deals with customers:

1. *The customer always comes first.* To say "the customer comes first" sounds simple. Almost everyone will agree that this is the way it should be, but too often companies forget this basic axiom. Many companies create bureaucracies; middle management engages in endless meetings with no speedy resolution to the pressing issues at hand, and, in the end, customer concerns are not dealt with in a reasonable amount of time.

It's up to the information professional to work with the salesperson if issues are not being quickly resolved through the usual channels. He should be able to count on the sales rep as his trusted emissary in such cases. The salesperson needs to know of any issues that are affecting the librarian's satisfaction (or dissatisfaction) with the service his company is providing, including issues unrelated to the sales relationship.

2. *The customer is always right.* This is another one of those basic business tenets that all of us have heard before and generally agree with. Yet there are times when companies must say "no" to a specific customer request, and, in these cases, it should be the goal of every service provider, in any industry, to provide an explanation as to why the customer's request cannot be fulfilled. As a former senior sales executive, I never liked to see a sales rep deliver bad news to his customer, but when a company simply cannot agree to what the customer is asking, the rep must be included in all communications to that effect.

3. *Even if we think the customer is wrong, we try to make them right.* When the company says "no," the rep should do everything possible to help the company say "yes." The rep and the information professional share a goal to have any issue or issues resolved. It is in both their best interests to work together to encourage the company to provide a solution to any and every customer concern or need. The sales rep must work behind the

scenes to explore every possible avenue to achieve a positive result for his customer.

4. Every decision we make in relation to our customer needs to be made by putting ourselves in the customer's place. The salesperson always needs to imagine how his customers feel about whatever problems they're having.

By following these four guidelines faithfully, we can avoid this end result: *If our customers are unhappy, we will eventually have no customers, and shortly thereafter we will have no business.*

The information industry is littered with examples of companies that took themselves too seriously, didn't put into practice customer satisfaction guidelines, or were acquired by inappropriate suitors and, as a result, found themselves either out of business or marginalized and forgotten. Success is like paying rent: Every 30 days the rent is due, and a company's success lasts only 30 days, as well.

Everyone in the company needs to know why its product offerings are important to the customers. Whether an employee works in the mailroom, purchasing, or IT, everyone and *anyone* in the company who draws a paycheck should know that their work is part of a company-wide effort to better serve the customer. If the customer is happy, there will be revenue coming in, and when revenue comes in, the company can continue to pay everyone's salary and benefits.

Salespeople need to think about how they personally would want to be treated as a customer and transfer that feeling to the way they treat information professionals.

Guidelines for the Information Professional

In these days of reduced resources for libraries, every dollar spent on resources is examined carefully. The organization employing the information professional wants to make sure its employees are up to dealing with vendors. They want to have confidence that the library staff who interact with vendors not only know the best sources for data but also have negotiation skills equal to the task of dealing with the many salespeople who come to the library to sell any number of products and services.

The truly successful information professional follows these guidelines:

1. **Know yourself:** While an MLIS degree focuses on the collection and dissemination of information, you also have a responsibility to maintain a library or information center that houses the best information sources available. Whether you like it or not, salespeople will beat a path to your door. Their job is to sell you something and your job is to decide whether to buy the product they are touting. You need to be up to the task: to meet, greet, ask probing questions, negotiate, and buy data from the salespeople. Engage in conversation with the sales reps. The more you interact, the more you will know.

2. **Set goals:** Your goals are similar to those of the salesperson: more money, a promotion, a desire to spend more quality time with your family. However, one additional goal that the information professional should have is to learn from the salesperson. How can you apply the lessons learned from the buying and selling process to your internal organization? Countless books have been written about the "internal sell," describing how to demonstrate in word and deed to upper management that you qualify for that pay raise or key promotion. Take mental notes of the sales process you go through with the reps you respect the most and apply those principles internally.

3. **Maintain leverage:** I will discuss this concept many times in the book since I feel that I cannot overstate the importance of the *customer's* leverage. Libraries represent a very profitable business for data providers,

and you are the target audience. If after reading this book you understand that, as a purchaser of information, you have enormous power to buy what you want at a reasonable price from the vendors you prefer to deal with, then this book will be worth whatever price you paid for it.

Not all the guidelines needed to be successful will be found in a book or in a course at the state university. Much of what must be learned inevitably will come from the old "learning by doing" axiom. Even a surgeon who thought that she had learned everything there is to know about her craft in med school actually becomes a better surgeon as she performs more operations. There is inherent knowledge, and there is knowledge gained as a result of trial and error. Observation of mentors and colleagues plus years of experience on the job shape the people we become in our chosen professions. We cannot know everything there is to know on the first day on the job. Although we must have some basic skills to initially work with, we learn by doing.

Having come to sales from a teaching and performing background, it was relatively easy for me to interact with all types of customers and prospects, and I was also extremely fortunate to have the benefit of mentors who were there for me in times of need. Library schools should take advantage of information industry veterans who have called on and serviced libraries throughout their careers to counsel aspiring librarians on the why, what, and how of working with vendor sales reps.

When I was a kid, my favorite baseball player was Mickey Mantle. I had a complete series of his baseball cards, and I went to as many Yankee games as possible just to see him play. I copied his batting stance when we played baseball in the park, emulated the way he ran the bases, and did everything I could to learn from the best. Sadly, my baseball skills were not on the same level as his and a baseball career was not in the cards for me. I was no Mickey Mantle.

In business, there are a number of companies in any given industry that are successful, acknowledged leaders. Whether it's the way they hire and train their employees or the talent and knowledge of their executive team or CEO, successful companies have always been emulated by those that intend to become successful. And why not?

Companies like Apple are not successful by coincidence. They have a tried and true methodology that they impart to every employee. The procedures followed in the New York Apple store are the same as those in a St. Louis mall. Everyone at Apple is working under a specific plan, and, as long as annual profits keep growing, the company will continue to train its employees accordingly. Wise businesspeople study companies like Apple and try to apply its methods to their own operations. Learning and copying techniques from the best is no crime, and, as a matter of fact, it is greatly encouraged in the business world.

When I was promoted to VP of sales for an information company, I began to work closely with a number of Wall Street information professionals. All of them employed significant numbers of librarians in their information centers to provide information services to company offices all over the world. Moreover, many held the title of VP and were compensated quite handsomely for their efforts. It was, and still is, a very impressive group of people.

In working closely with these librarians, I quickly realized how important their relationships with our salespeople were to them. Often, a senior executive needed data immediately, and it was critical that our rep respond to his need without delay. Because of the value of the service we provided to these libraries, our renewal rate was the highest in the industry.

I also noticed that these customers encouraged salespeople (and not just ours) to come in regularly and present new products and services to their staffs. They knew what products they wanted and were fierce negotiators on price for new acquisitions and also at renewal time. Visiting these firms and meeting with their librarians was both challenging and rewarding; clearly, the librarians realized that the salesperson represented an opportunity for them to bring in the latest information technologies and products, which in turn increased the librarians' value to their firms. It was a quid quo pro relationship that served both the rep and the librarian well.

Obviously, the information needs of a Wall Street investment firm are different from the needs of an academic library, which in turn are different from those of a public library. The end result, however, is the same. The library provides information services to help its patrons make informed decisions. The quality of those decisions is directly based on the quality of the resources provided to the library's constituency. The salesperson can help the information professional obtain the highest quality data sources, so actively communicating with the sales rep benefits the librarian and his entire organization.

The information professional needs to try to help the sales rep understand the inner workings of the library. For instance, she might say to the rep:

- This is our short-term (or long-term) strategy.

- The library director wants us to follow this course of action in order to build certain collections.

- We must adhere to the following purchasing procedures.

- We issue an RFP every 3 years for general reference products; the next one will be released next winter.

- Decisions on purchasing are made by a group of three people at the library including the library director, who gets final approval from her boss. The process can take up to 6 months.

In the end, there are a host of questions that need to be answered and addressed by both the librarian and sales rep. It takes time for trust to be established, for bonds to develop, and for relationships to flourish.

Persistence

Many times, between the initial presentation and the final closing of the sale, we are faced with a choice of persevering or backing down. Thomas Alva Edison may have said it best when he declared that "Our greatest weakness lies in giving up."

As a key element of their skill set, persistence is highly regarded by sales reps. For every significant order, the road to success is riddled with land mines, such as poor timing, declining budgets, and prospects with no influence to buy resources. Salespeople are often left wondering when that big order will finally arrive. Smart salespeople know that in order to be successful they have to exercise both patience and careful persistence. The goal of virtually all training exercises for sales reps is to do everything possible to eliminate the guesswork regarding when the order will arrive. This is done through carefully planned methodologies based on the understanding that an order doesn't just appear out of the sky.

Information professionals know about persistence as well. Given that the organizations they work for expect them to follow the latest industry trends, to be familiar with competing products, and to negotiate the best possible financial deal with the vendor, the word *persistence* is part of an information professional's daily vernacular.

When I became national sales director for the academic library market early in my career, I was thrilled to plan my first trip to California, since the state was home to so many universities in my target market (i.e., schools with business programs). The company I represented had a product that was perfect for these institutions.

During that first trip and in the years that followed, I called on virtually every major university on the west coast that had an MBA program, with all but one of these institutions becoming customers. The one that continually eluded my efforts not only wouldn't buy; they wouldn't even consent to a sales meeting. No matter what I said or how I said it, the customer was unavailable, and I was told I should call again on my next west coast trip.

On one such subsequent trip, I called my contact at this university again and explained that I had an appointment at another office on campus directly across the street from her library. Once again, I was rebuffed, but while declining to meet, she said I could leave information about the product with the person at the reference desk. I left an information packet with a personalized price sheet for suggested subscriptions applicable to an institution like hers and then dutifully followed up by email upon my return to New York. I did not hear back.

Approximately 6 months later, I received a letter in the mail from my elusive contact at the university, along with the product list I'd left for her. She had circled a number of subscriptions she wanted to buy and added up their collective cost. The subscriptions she'd chosen totaled approximately $29,000, which represented a very significant order from an academic institution at that time. A purchase order was also included; all I had to do was process it.

However, our pricing to academic institutions included a volume discount, meaning that the more elements of the product ordered, the lower the price per unit. In other words, what my customer had circled were *a la carte* options, when in fact she could have gotten the much less costly *prix fixe*. Her $29,000 order, when I recalculated it, could be had for $23,500. At this point I had a moral dilemma. I could put the order through as written and give her a magical discount on her renewal the following year, or I could call her and explain our pricing scheme, and risk losing the order altogether. I knew immediately what I had to do.

I had persistently called on this person for the better part of 2 years before finally gaining her business. Taking the high road now was the only way to go if I wanted to build a productive and long-standing business relationship. I called her and explained that her total price was actually lower than the price on her purchase order. She thanked me and amended the order for the lesser price.

I closed the sale soon thereafter, and a few months later she agreed to see me on my next trip to her city.

Because of my persistence and my concern for the customer, this person and I became the best of friends for many years. I was told by other west coast librarians that I was the only salesperson she consistently welcomed into her library.

The best salespeople are not only persistent but also have a clear focus on providing their library customers with a quality product that serves their patrons' needs. They need to understand that the approval process at libraries today is a protracted one and to be aware of the many people involved in the approval process. But getting back to persistence, we all know that sometimes a persistent individual may be considered pushy or, even worse, someone who "won't take no for an answer." If the information professional believes that the salesperson's persistence is bordering on unacceptable, then that dissatisfaction needs to be communicated initially to the rep and, if it continues, to the company:

> "Alan, thank you for calling me. As I previously indicated, while your product seems to be excellent, I cannot make a buying decision at the present time. You really need not call me every week as you have been for the last month. I should have more information for you in 2 months."

By setting clear guidelines as to when the rep may or may not call, the information professional establishes the ground rules of communication.

The "signals" buyers provide to sellers regarding their interest in continuing the process may not always be clear or easily read. If the information professional has no intention of purchasing a particular product, then it is his responsibility to simply state that fact. If the librarian believes he has been clear on this point and feels harassed by an overly persistent salesperson, then he is well within his rights to bring the offensive behavior to the rep's attention and instruct him to back off.

In the example of my reluctant west coast librarian, her inability (or unwillingness) to speak with me directly seriously prolonged the buying and selling process. It would have been helpful if she'd spoken with me early on and explained that although she could not see me right away, she was interested and I should continue trying to contact her. Fortunately, I was pleasantly persistent in that case—mainly because I felt so strongly that my product would be useful to the university's business school. I like to think that I was focused *and* persistent in this situation, in a nice way.

Honesty is defined as the quality, condition, or characteristic of being fair, truthful, and morally upright, while *persistence* is defined as the quality of continuing steadily despite problems or difficulties. One can certainly be both honest and persistent. It was the combination of those two traits that helped me cement the relationship between my company and the west coast client. It took time, but the end result was worth it. Careful persistence helped me close the order, and honesty helped keep it closed for many profitable years.

It is important for a sales rep to understand the difference between "careful persistence" and just plain persistence. Some sales organizations simply encourage their salespeople to be persistent. That's understandable, but an overly zealous sales rep may take it too far, and you can't sell a product if you've upset your prospective customer. In my many years of dealing with library folks, I've seen that high pressure tactics by sales reps almost never work.

A salesperson walks a fine line between the customer and the company. Yes, products need to be sold and the rep is the person who needs to sell them. However, the rep is also tasked to work directly with the information professional to establish a close bond between the vendor and the library. It's hard to establish such a bond when, in the name of persistence, reps are overly aggressive in their communications with the librarian. The information professional should remember that she is in control of the relationship and can set the ground rules for communication. If a librarian feels at any time that the rep is being overly zealous or stubborn, or just becoming a general pain in the neck, she has the right and the responsibility to set him straight.

Let's look at an example to illustrate this. On the vendor side, a sales manager had been told by sales rep Susan that an order would come in by a certain time, and, to date, it hadn't appeared. The sales manager had to present his team's revenue projections to his boss, so he pressured Susan to check with her library contact to ascertain where the order was being held up and push for completion, at which point Susan contacted the library director instead of her contact, a show of disrespect.

This was the response Susan received:

> "Susan, I didn't appreciate your constant calling, especially when you contacted my boss directly. I'm your contact here, and as I've already said, no decision has been made. When it is, I'll call you."

What happened here?

The salesperson went through the process of qualifying the account, making the appointment, visiting the library, and presenting the product, but then found herself in the uncomfortable position of waiting for her contact to give a "yea" or "nay" on buying the product. The sales rep was expecting a decision by a specific time. When seemingly no decision had been made as of that date, the librarian opted not to say anything at all.

In this case, both the information professional and the sales rep failed to do their jobs adequately. Where timing on follow-up has been mutually agreed to, the information professional has a responsibility to keep the sales rep informed of the status of the approval. Under these circumstances, silence is not a viable communication option. Susan was wrong to try to circumvent her contact at the library—that never works. In short, mutual expectations in relation to timing were not met or clearly communicated.

By working together in a persistent and transparent manner, both the salesperson and the librarian can achieve their mutual goals and help one another. Many times in my career, I presented a product and was told that funding approval was not imminent. The librarian might tell me, for example, that there was a chance of funding in 6 months. I'd make a note of this in my follow-up file, and, 6 months later to the day, I'd call the librarian to ask if the funding had come through. Sometimes I was greeted with the good news that, in fact, funding for the product had been approved; more often, my call served as a friendly reminder for my contact at the library to follow up on the approval process. Either way, when both parties are carefully persistent and rigorous about follow-up, it will lead to the best possible result for everyone involved.

In some companies, there are salespeople tasked solely with servicing major accounts. These accounts are usually customers whose level of spending is considerably higher than average. Some companies refer to such customers as the "Million Dollar Group," the "Big Guys," or "MVAs" (as I talked about in Chapter 1). Whatever you call them, no company can afford to overlook their importance.

It is extremely important for the vendor to keep a steady line of communication open with the libraries in this select group to ensure their satisfaction and to make sure they maintain their level of commitment to the company's products. At one company where I had this role, I was required to see my major accounts every 90 days. To ensure that this occurred, at the conclusion of a meeting with the customer, I would suggest scheduling a return appointment in 90 days:

> "Thanks for seeing me today, Joanne," I might say. "I'm glad I was able to show you our latest databases and answer your questions."

"I appreciate the time you've spent with me at our new library" would be a typical response.

"So, today is January 12. I'd like to meet with you again on April 12, if that works for you."

"I'm really not sure—that's so far off."

"If you're okay with penciling it in, as we approach the date, I'll call to confirm."

In all the times I attempted to arrange the advanced schedule like this, no one ever said "no." Customers are happy to see that there is a commitment on the part of the company to their continued satisfaction.

KNOWLEDGE POINTS

- The customer is always right.

- As Paul Simon wrote and sang with Art Garfunkel, "Keep the customer satisfied." Great song; greater message.

- An unhappy customer is no customer.

- The information professional needs to recognize the value of the sales rep as a provider of the latest technologies, an advisor on industry trends, and someone who can provide the most bang for the library's buck. The information professional should work to make the salesperson a friend of the library.

- Librarians have goals they need to achieve, whether it's to get the best new databases or weed out information sources that have failed to satisfy their constituencies.

- Librarians may have to wait years for funding in order to purchase a specific data source. By lobbying library management to approve important purchases, and staying the course until their objectives are met, information professionals practice persistence to achieve the library's goals.

- For the sales rep, it's easier to gain a customer than to keep a customer, and it's hard to close an order but harder to keep it closed. If the sales rep works to earn the info pro's respect through consistent, quality service over time, the rep will come to be regarded as someone who can be depended on for the best products at the most reasonable price.

- It is important for a sales rep to understand the difference between "careful persistence" and just plain persistence.

- The information professional needs to encourage a dialogue with the salesperson, because only through communication can their mutual goals be met.

Making the Most of Trade Shows

In the tune "Limelight," sung and written by Rush, there is the line, "All the world's indeed a stage, and we are merely players, performers and portrayers, each another's audience, outside the gilded cage." I think of trade shows as stage settings for salespeople to interact with customers and prospects alike. You could almost liken a trade show to "participatory theater."

It's safe to say that trade shows are a declining business. Just look around the exhibit hall at the last trade show you attended. Reduced travel funds for salespeople and librarians have shrunk the attendance levels for both. Associations that sponsor these shows have run out of original ideas to attract new vendors. Moreover, given the shrinking attendance, fewer sales seem to occur as a result of these shows, so, in turn, even shows in which vendors have participated for many years are being cut out of the budget. CEOs, finance directors, and sales VPs are under constant pressure to reexamine their company's trade show direction to save money.

There is no question that times are changing in relation to trade shows and that we all need to better understand how to make these meetings viable for everyone. However, let's not throw out the baby with the bath water.

The Importance of Trade Shows

Trade shows are a fundamental part of the sales cycle and customer relationship development. For the sales rep, they can mean long but productive days of meeting with important clients or potential customers. For the information professional, the show can represent easy, one-stop shopping and the opportunity to meet with all types of reps, compare products and services, and see the latest and greatest in product development—all in 3 to 4 days.

Trade shows provide an equal opportunity for the vendor and the customer to efficiently connect. According to the Center for Exhibit Industry Research (CEIR; www.ceir.org), more than 85 percent of the trade show audience is made up of final decision makers or those who influence purchases. Translated, this means that salespeople have an opportunity to present themselves to decision makers and influencers all day long. These people are coming in to see not only the salesperson but also senior executives, marketing people, and customer care representatives. Trade show attendance by information professionals can be a learning experience as well as a buying experience.

Other statistics from CEIR indicate that 91 percent of attendees believe trade shows are the number one source of information to help them make purchasing decisions. At trade shows, attendees are able to directly compare many products in a category at one location. In other words, they can see all the products they want to buy from multiple vendors on the same day. This is reason enough for buyers to go to trade shows, but here are some reasons from CEIR for salespeople to attend as well:

- An average of 81 percent to 83 percent of visitors has some kind of buying power.

- The average visitor spends 9.2 hours at the exhibit hall at a 2 to 3 day trade show.

- Of the visitors coming to the booth, 86 percent will be new contacts.

- For up to 10 weeks after the show, 77 percent of visitors will remember your company.

Of course, there are some attendees at trade shows who go only for the vendor events, local sightseeing, and meals with friends and relatives. As a result, some of those who ostensibly go to trade shows for professional development never set foot in the exhibit hall or attend a professional session. Unfortunately for those folks, they are missing opportunities to learn. The good news is that the majority of librarians who attend these shows spend considerable time in the exhibit hall.

The true opportunity for both the salesperson and the information professional is to use this time to be visible, be present, and connect. Sure, the attendees will network with their colleagues away from the hall, and of course they will do some sightseeing and maybe even play some golf. Sometimes the exhibit hall will seem like the loneliest spot on the planet. But the people who do show up in the exhibit hall are the ones that want to see a salesperson and learn more about the products.

It comes down to focus once again. If information professionals focus on what products they want to see and which companies they want to visit, then their time spent at the show will be worthwhile. Trade show attendees should create a list of all the vendors they want to see as well as a corresponding map and schedule. Following the map and schedule will allow them to see everyone on their list in a reasonable amount of time. To make the process even smoother, they should make appointments with the vendors of choice prior to the show. An information professional might say the following:

> "Bill, I'll be at the conference on Tuesday, July 14. I'd like to stop by the booth to see you at 3:00 PM. Are you available for a meeting? I'd like to discuss our upcoming renewal with you. If your boss is there, that would be even better, as I have some suggestions I'd like to share with the management of your company."

Selling to or Becoming a Serious Buyer

I have a friend who once sold real estate. One of his jobs involved the selling of new condominiums that were located somewhat off the beaten path. Although they were beautiful units, not too many people showed up to see them because of the location. He reasoned that anyone who would make the effort to find the place and actually show up was a better than average prospect.

He immediately knew that he had motivated buyers when a couple would show up on a rainy Sunday afternoon to look at the units being sold. Similarly, most of the people who go to the trouble to come to trade shows are serious and motivated buyers.

Salespeople need to remember that there are several types of people who will walk through an exhibit booth or want to meet with a rep. These include the casual participant who just wants to be "in the know" but has no intention of buying. Then there is the person collecting information to better understand the available choices. Finally, most important to the sales rep is the serious buyer.

An information professional who is a serious buyer should come to the exhibit hall with a list of questions. Serious buyers have done their initial homework on what they want to purchase or know what problems they are trying to solve. Many times, they have contacted the salesperson before the show to arrange a specific meeting time. Often the rep will arrange for a high-level executive of the company to be part of the meeting. This is the best example of how salespeople and librarians should get together at trade shows.

In this situation, the information professional already knows which vendors to see and plans the days accordingly. A trade show is the best place for serious buyers to see demonstrations of products they may want to buy before making a commitment as well as to compare similar products offered by competing vendors. In one afternoon, a serious buyer at a trade show can see three or more competitive products and then make a decision on which one to buy. The serious buyers know why they are there.

Of course, there are other trade show attendees who are not so well organized. There are people who just want to go the many booths and pick up free pens, sticky notes, or chocolate. However, there is always room for these browsers; it is important for the salespeople to still pay some attention to the "non-buyers" because they are potential customers.

Although a majority of the giveaways at booths are picked up by non-buyers, the point is that all these people will take those pens and sticky notes back to their libraries. A pen on a desk or a sticky note at the reference desk with the company's name is good advertising. It contributes to the company's brand recognition.

Preparing for a Trade Show

The bottom line is that the majority of attendees who come to the trade show will browse, review, or make buying decisions or recommendations. So how can the librarian and the salesperson make the most of these opportunities to connect? By learning the art of trade show preparation.

Tips for the Salesperson

Salespeople need to look to their companies for direction as to why they should attend a particular trade show. Possible answers to "What are our objectives for attending the trade show?" can be as diverse as:

- A new product is being introduced.

- All the major competitors are there as well as our customers.

- The current CEO has resigned, or a new CEO has joined the company and wants to meet key customers.

- A new company is being acquired.

Whatever the reasons, the sales staff needs to understand why the company is exhibiting and attending. What are the goals for the show? If everyone knows the goals and objectives, then the show will have meaning and purpose. Other than sales and marketing staff, who else from the company is attending and why? Salespeople should know what purpose everyone who attends will serve at the show. What measures will be used to determine if the show was a success? In order to accomplish the objectives, it's important for sales staff to know in advance what criteria will be used in the post-show analysis to determine whether the goals were accomplished.

Before a certain trade show I attended, a major prospective customer indicated that he wanted to see me to review a new database my company had introduced. As always, I made appointments in advance to see key customers and prospects at the show. We settled on a time during the first day of the show. The appointment time came and went, but the customer was a no-show. He called me that night to apologize, and we agreed to a breakfast meeting on the last day of the show. But I was stood up again.

When the show was over, we were packing up the booth and the literature amidst a sea of noise and impatient vendors and salespeople rushing to try to catch their transportation home. Suddenly, in walked my prospect accompanied by his wife, both of them professors at a local major university.

"Mike, am I too late?" he asked, rushing into the bedlam of the hall.

Keeping my composure, I slit open the carton I had just sealed, took out some brochures, and flipped open my laptop in one smooth motion. We spoke for probably another 5 minutes above the noise. At the end of the conversation, he said to me, "Mike, send me whatever forms I need so I can buy the product." This situation worked in my favor because I was still prepared for the meeting. My prospect had every intention of meeting with me. It was just that his organizational skills were somewhat lacking.

Making appointments prior to the trade show is important for both the customer and the rep, even if they don't always go as planned.

Before any salesperson is allowed the privilege of attending a trade show where scores of prospects are expected, sales management needs to know if the rep has properly prepared for the show. They can know this by reviewing the number of appointments arranged by each rep in advance of the show. If a rep has fewer than five confirmed appointments, he simply should not be permitted to attend. Many presidents of companies and VPs of sales require a specific number of appointments for every trade show attended by their sales staff. The company is committing a significant amount of money to attend a trade show and therefore has an obligation to properly prepare sales staff for the show. It is also expected that senior sales executives will be present at the booth to meet and greet customers and participate in the scheduled meetings. If senior sales executives are not at the booth for part of the day, something is amiss. The most important location for senior management at a trade show is at the booth.

Salespeople will almost always be successful at trade shows when they have planned appointments in advance of the show; some of those appointments should also include senior executives, technical people, and customer care representatives.

Here is a summary of the important things for a sales professional to remember regarding trade shows:

- Know ahead of time which of your customers or prospective customers will be attending, and set up appointments with those you need to see.

- Know your audience, as many trade shows are segmented by library type.

- Be knowledgeable about your competition, and make sure you know if any big product announcements are being made by them.

- Schedule time away from the booth for key prospects and customers, as it's often hard to have a serious one-on-one conversation in the exhibit hall.

- Attend association seminars at the show to learn about the industry; you may even meet a key prospect or customer at one of those sessions.

Tips for the Information Professional

Buyers of information likewise benefit from trade shows when they arrange appointments with key vendors in advance of the show. It's all about planning, including the following steps:

- Know ahead of time what vendors you want to visit.

- Prepare your questions.

- If you want to speak with a particular individual, make an appointment for a specific date and time.

- Devise a road map of the exhibition hall so you can navigate the floor more easily.

- RSVP to vendor events prior to the show.

- Ask for a one-on-one demo of the products you are interested in.

KNOWLEDGE POINTS

- Trade shows make sense for both the buyer and the seller.

- For both the buyer and the seller, carefully planned appointments are a necessity.

- Vendors need to set clear goals and objectives for every staff member attending the show.

- Libraries and information centers need to set clear goals and objectives for the library staff attending the show.

- The fact that trade show attendance is on the decline doesn't mean that salespeople and librarians should abandon this important opportunity for face-to-face communication; rather, both parties have to be more efficient and focused in activities at trade shows to ensure success.

CHAPTER

The Importance of Your Words

♪ "It's only words, and words are all I have to take your heart away," sang The Bee Gees in "Words" written by Barry, Maurice, and Robin Gibb. The song presents a good sentiment for those hoping for romance, but in business relationships, we have to downplay hope and use our words effectively.

"You can't make this stuff up." I'm sure all of us at one time or another have uttered this phrase in shocked disbelief when our friends, neighbors, or elected officials have said something ridiculous for everyone to hear or sent an inappropriate email for everyone to read. We outwardly laugh, but inside we are incredulous.

I am a strong proponent of the written and spoken word and take the responsibility of being absolutely sure the words I write and speak are in good taste and not offensive. All experienced professionals in any industry know that successful business relationships depend on a better-than-average command of written and spoken communication. Inherent in that skill is understanding the content of what is being written and choosing your words carefully.

What Not to Put in Writing

Our society is entranced by immediate communication. Millions of emails, tweets, instant messages, and texts are sent every day.

Instant communication is pervasive in our daily lives. We contact each other literally at the speed of light. However, sometimes in communication speed can be dangerous

While speedy communication is important, taking time to think about your words may be more important. It is almost never a great idea to email or text another person when you are angry or agitated. After emailing or texting in the heat of the moment, even if you apologize or say that you really didn't mean it, the damage has been done. The offended party may re-read that inflammatory email over and over again.

I have counseled many a sales rep to not send any email response in anger, and I would give the same advice to information professionals as well. The best way to handle an explosive situation that cries out for an email response is to write a message but not immediately send it. Wait 24 hours and then read it again. Putting some distance between writing it, thinking about it, and sending it provides time to cool down. On further examination a day later, you can probably amend the language so that the email still gets the point across but does not offend the receiver.

Many real-life situations occur that reinforce this lesson. In the category of "You can't make this stuff up," here is a situation that I recently witnessed first-hand.

My wife is a healthcare professional. She recently decided that she would prefer part-time work as opposed to working 40+ hours per week. She contacted a number of recruiters and, as expected, began to get inquiries about her availability. One such communication suggested that she consider selling healthcare products and services to her friends, family, and neighbors. For my wife to become a salesperson is as unlikely as for me to examine a medical patient. She doesn't want to do what I do for living, and I don't want to do what she does for a living. In short, the prospect of her even thinking about a sales career is slim to none.

But because she is naturally a thorough person, and because of her medical training, she decided to investigate a possible new road of employment in a sales capacity. She was contacted about a sales opportunity to be conducted from home. She read the printed materials, listened to the WebEx presentation describing her duties, and then followed up with the person who originally contacted her by phone to tell him that she was not interested.

Their phone conversation was brief, businesslike, and professional. All seemed finished until she received the following email from the person she had spoken to on the phone the day before. I have not altered the email in any way. Only the names have been eliminated. Again, I couldn't make this up if I tried:

> incredible,
>
> you now have knowledge in your hands that can dramatically effect 100's if not 1000's of people in your circle
>
> and you choose to do nothing with it.
>
> that is terribly short sighted and all because the business model says more to you than a life changing discovery.
>
> just awful … and incredibly selfish.

This is a graphic example of inappropriate choices of words, a message written in the heat of the moment without much thought of the consequences. It makes the writer look foolish, and its tone of desperation is a poor reflection on the way the company's business is conducted. It would have been a lot smarter for the writer to review the email a day or two later and not send it out at all.

If you're angry, don't immediately convey that feeling in writing. What you write will reflect on you, and, just as important, will make an impression on the person receiving the email, who is still considering doing business with your organization. Personal recommendations are a significant part of acquiring new business. I know my wife will never recommend this company's products to her friends and associates.

Communicating Honestly

In the world of buying and selling, honest communication can mean the difference between completing a sale or delaying or even sabotaging the sale. A good salesperson chooses his words wisely, and the informed librarian knows what words to listen for.

People sometimes use words to mislead the other party, and in the sales world, this can lead to a failed business relationship. I recently decided to buy a new car, specifically a convertible. The first car I bought at age 22 was a convertible. It was my first and only ragtop, and I liked to feel the breezes blowing through my hair as I cruised down the highway. Of course, getting a convertible at my current age means the wind will be whizzing around my bald head. Nevertheless, I prepared myself for the process of buying a new car, a process that causes many of us to cringe, as we realize some car salespeople are rightly given their notorious reputation.

After some perfunctory analysis of car performance reports, I narrowed the search to a particular brand and model. At a local dealership, I was told that I was in luck—there was a "Sales Manager's Special" available that day. Apparently, it was the car driven by the sales manager the previous year, and it had low mileage and what the dealer assured me was a reasonable price. It was even a color that I liked, so I test drove it. I was delighted with all the features included for what I thought was an attractive price. I thanked the salesperson for her time spent with me, and then decided to go home and do some further research before making the commitment to buy. I promised to call the sales rep the next day with questions and comments.

Going back to my research that night, I noticed that the Blue Book price for the model and year in question was considerably lower than the price being quoted by the dealership. The next day, I dutifully called the salesperson and questioned the price she had given me the day before, expecting her to offer some accommodation. Her explanation for the price differential was that the car, although driven more than 7,000 miles by the sales manager, was never registered, and therefore the dealership classified it as a new car, not a used one. What they were calling "new" was actually "used" as far as I was concerned.

Paying a new car price for a used car was not an option for me. As a result, neither the salesperson nor I got what we wanted. The car sat in the lot unsold, I didn't get a car, the salesperson didn't get a commission—in all, a lose–lose situation.

When a database salesperson is speaking to a librarian, the goal is to create an atmosphere that will lend itself to a win–win situation, where both the seller and the buyer get something they want. Similarly, when the librarian approaches a salesperson, that same atmosphere of trying to achieve a mutually beneficial outcome is necessary. The seller wants to sell and the buyer wants to buy. It's as simple as that. To achieve success, both participants need to speak with honesty and conviction:

> "Bill, I heard that your new aerospace database has serious bugs in it. If I make the purchase decision, will you and the company stand behind your offer of a full refund?" a librarian might ask.
>
> "Of course we will. I know the bugs are minor and being addressed as we speak," the salesperson might respond. "You have my assurance that it will work for you, but if you're still uncomfortable, we can write those refund terms into the order form. It's my job to make sure that you are a satisfied customer."

In this case, both parties spoke with honesty and conviction. Whether the customer buys or not, the salesperson has established an atmosphere of professionalism and trust. Those are good conditions for the two parties to come to an agreement.

The Words You Choose Make a Difference

The information industry resides in a continuously changing environment. Today's exotic, boundary-breaking, game-changing technology is forgotten tomorrow. New terminology, new acronyms, and names of new communication devices have to be learned daily. When making buying and selling decisions, both the salesperson and the information professional must understand the terminology.

But it's not always just new terminology that can cause a misunderstanding. The sometimes casual and inconsistent use of common words can negate all the hard work leading up to the moment of agreement. Here is an example of a typical conversation at the close of a sale:

> "It's just about time to sign the contract," the sales rep informs the librarian.
>
> "Gee, Bob I don't know if I have the legal authority or responsibility to sign a contract," the librarian may respond. "Looks like a lot of legalese. I'll need another opinion before I can even think about signing this."

Upon hearing the phrase "sign the contract," the librarian suddenly is apprehensive about committing. Many people associate the word *contract* with legal matters. Buying a car, buying a house, or making any major purchase usually involves some sort of onerous contract with numerous places to sign on multipage documents, with spaces reserved for many signatures. ("Just sign here and there and initial here, and don't forget to sign on the back, check the box marked under severe penalty ...")

It does not evoke pleasant memories, does it? Why would a sales rep want a prospective customer to be reminded of past unpleasant experiences when buying an information product? In some cases, the prospect of making a major monetary purchase that requires multiple signatures can overwhelm anyone with worry. The more money involved in the purchase, the more likely lawyers will be involved as well.

A different choice of words could be all it takes to avoid evoking all these unpleasant thoughts. For example, a far more appealing phrase at closing would be "Authorize the order form." The word *authorize* implies the power is with the person signing, in other words, that she has the power to get the deal done. The term *order form* also conveys power, as the word *order* clearly implies the action taken is in the hands of the buyer. Another more empowering choice of words would be "Can I have your signature on the form so we can finalize this purchase?" When the salesperson shares the power with the customer, both parties feel in control.

Just consider the difference between the following statements:

> The sales rep at XYZ Data sold me a database about archeology.

or

> I bought a new database about archeology from XYZ Data.

They're talking about the same outcome, but the second statement tells the listener that both the sales rep and the info pro were part of the buying and selling process, as should always be the goal.

KNOWLEDGE POINTS

- Whether a sales rep or info pro, always think before you speak or write.

- Never send an email, text, or tweet in anger. If you write it and send it, you can't deny what was written. Give yourself a day to calm down before sending it.

- When salespeople and librarians engage, both parties need to communicate honestly, in order to create a win–win situation.

- Sales reps should choose words that empower a customer in the purchasing process, not words that connote negative thoughts.

TWO

THE SALES MEETING

The brilliant song "Keep the Customer Satisfied," written by Paul Simon and performed by Simon & Garfunkel, may very well be telling the woeful journey of a salesperson whose attempts at selling something are continually thwarted. When the information professional and the salesperson understand how they can work together, everyone will profit from the experience and no one will exit empty handed.

In this section, I'll cover everything sales reps and info pros need to know about the sales meeting.

The first topic discussed is how both the sales rep and the librarian should prepare for their meetings. The rationale for including this information comes from analyzing and reviewing the many sales meetings that I have participated in over the years as a salesperson and a manager. I have met with countless information professionals at libraries throughout the world. From candid conversations I've had with MLS students, sales executives, and library directors, it's clear to me that the skill set involved in preparing, negotiating, and concluding discussions with salespeople tends to be a sensitive area. The information in this section of the book will help the librarian be better prepared for any meetings/negotiations and will also provide some valuable insight into how the salesperson prepares for the meeting.

There are different kinds of meetings that accomplish a variety of tasks as the buyer and seller travel down the road to purchasing a product or service. I will examine the meaning of those meetings and suggest techniques to help both parties focus on the tasks at hand. A meeting for the sake of meeting benefits no one. In order for both the rep and the librarian to reach a productive and efficient outcome, for the mutual benefit of both parties, everyone's role needs to be appreciated and understood.

This section also covers the use of an agenda for each meeting and provides time management suggestions that are relevant to both salespeople and library professionals.

I also describe what a typical sales meeting should look like: what to say, what not to say, and how the negotiation process works for both the sales rep and information professional.

For me, one of the most interesting aspects about being a salesperson for all these years is the fact that no two sales meetings were ever the same. Much like Scrabble or poker, where every game is unique, every sales meeting is also different. Just because a rep has presented the same product to similar libraries does not mean that the next sales meeting will be the same, and, most definitely, the results will always be different.

However, when a sales rep has presented a specific product over a long period of time, the rep becomes familiar with virtually all the questions related to that product. This expertise is most helpful for the information professional, because there is no question related to the product that the rep cannot answer. Part of building the librarian–sales rep relationship is the process of using each other as resources to determine whether the company's products are, in fact, a good fit for the library. In some cases, the product offered by the reps' company may not be as appropriate as the competition's, but an honest relationship between the two parties will help both sides come to the most logical conclusion as to what the library should buy and for how much.

Personalities, products, and places all serve to make each sales meeting a unique experience for all the parties involved. There are, however, structures and preparations that must remain the same. By adhering to a regimen of careful preparation, both the rep and the librarian have a better-than-average chance of achieving their individual goals and objectives. By understanding how the sales meeting will ultimately unfold, the information professional has an insight into the mindset of the salesperson. Similarly, if the salesperson can get an insight into the inner workings of the library, then that mutual flow of information will benefit both parties.

This section also includes advice on evaluating features and benefits of information products, and it concludes with a chapter that addresses possible barriers to an agreement. All of this information is designed to help the librarian be better prepared when the sales rep comes to visit.

Preparing for a Sales Meeting

"Wishin' and Hopin" was a huge hit for British songstress Dusty Springfield in 1964. Written by Burt Bacharach and Hal David, it remains one of their most enduring songs. However, neither the sales rep nor the information professional should rely merely on wishing or hoping when preparing for and participating in a sales meeting. In the arena of buying and selling information, the more that is left to chance, the greater the possibility of unfulfilled expectations for both parties.

By setting clear goals and expectations for a sales meeting, a salesperson can make the most of a sales meeting and develop a mutually beneficial relationship with the information professional.

On the other side of the table, an information professional is responsible for ensuring that the money requested and spent on buying databases, technology, equipment, consulting services, and other electronic resources is invested wisely. Before any expenditure is approved, information professionals should be familiar with the product being presented and confident that it will meet their needs (e.g., capabilities, ease of use, and, of course, cost). Even more importantly, the library administration needs to have confidence that the information professionals will conduct a thorough investigation before selecting a product and are well versed in negotiating its purchase.

A Well-Planned Sales Meeting

A sales meeting at a library is the result of careful planning. Salespeople are taught that time is money; time wasted is time that can never be brought back. The most successful salespeople are those who use time wisely. If a sales rep calls the library with the intent of discussing a product or service for consideration, the librarian should assume that the sales rep has researched the library's holdings and concluded that, at the very least, her company has a product that should complement the library's collections and is a possible candidate for purchase. Thus there is a bona fide reason to arrange a meeting. At the very least, there is cause for an initial discussion to explore the possibilities.

The librarian's responsibility in preparing for the sales meeting is to first determine if the product described by the rep is really germane to the library's mission. If it is, the next step is to schedule a convenient time for the librarian and rep to meet. It is preferable to meet somewhere away from the reference desk so that the time spent together is uninterrupted. The information professional should come to that first meeting familiar with the product to be discussed as well as other similar products.

To make the meeting as productive as possible for both parties, the information professional should ask the salesperson for an agenda in advance to set the topics to be discussed, clarify the objectives, and confirm the time and date. Both parties will benefit from this extra step. Reviewing an agenda in advance guarantees that there is a mutually understood purpose to the meeting. No one has the time for a pointless meeting.

The information professional should practice the Three C's:

- **Be concise:** Know what you want. "I want to see all databases related to nuclear energy. I don't want to spend more than $10,000 on any one of them. I want the data available for the entire library network throughout the world, 24/7."

- **Be clear:** Relate your needs clearly to the salesperson. "John, have I made it clear what it is I need from your company? Are we on the same page, because if we're not, let's go over it again just to be sure. Can you fulfill my needs based on the budget I have outlined?"

- **Be current:** Make sure you are well versed in the various aspects of the product to be presented and up to date on the latest technologies in the industry.

By putting into practice the Three C's, the information professional has taken the first step in preparing for the sales meeting. Of course, that is only the beginning of the long and sometimes bumpy road to making a purchase, but it is the best way to begin the journey.

For a salesperson to efficiently fill the information professional's needs, both parties need to be on the same page and, most importantly, on the same team. The reality is that the two of you are working together to get the best possible information sources into the library at the most reasonable cost. The information professional wants to put the salesperson in a position where she can help both people achieve the set objectives. It can be a classic win–win situation if both parties work together.

One way the info pro can strengthen the relationship is to inform the rep about the library's procedures for working with other departments. For example, if an academic librarian is considering a business-related database, will that librarian support the rep in also calling on the dean of the business school to gain additional demand for the product? When meeting with the librarian at an investment bank, is it advisable for the rep also to call on other departments, such as the mergers and acquisitions group? There is strength in numbers. The more areas in an organization that can benefit from buying a valid source of reliable information, the better, and seeking additional support will ultimately reinforce the work being done to provide world-class information for your organization.

Prior to every meeting of importance, the salesperson must supply an agenda to the customer. The information professional needs to review the agenda and return it to the sales rep, with additions and deletions, a few days before the meeting is to take place. Furthermore, if there will be any additional participants from either side, that information must be included.

In one of its early ad campaigns, Holiday Inn used the slogan: "The best surprise is no surprise." This holds true for the world of buying and selling as well. Knowing who will be joining a meeting is relevant to the discussion to take place. Including the ultimate decision-maker from either side helps the approval process move more smoothly. And if each side can somehow bring in the ultimate decision-makers, an enormous amount of time can be saved, mutual goals can be achieved, and everyone will benefit.

Here is a checklist of things information professionals should remember when planning to meet a salesperson:

- Be on time and arrange to meet in a quiet place.

- Speak with honesty and conviction.

- Know all the products that can meet your library's needs.

- Express the library's needs and clarify your objectives.

- Visit the vendor's website before the meeting to look for such things as product reviews, new product release dates, and acquisitions of new data sources.

- Understand the dynamics of a typical sales meeting.

- Respect the salesperson's time.

- Coach the salesperson on navigating your organization's decision-making process.

And here are some guidelines for sales representatives for planning on their end:

- Arrive 15 minutes before the scheduled meeting.

- Speak with honesty and conviction.

- Know your product line and be able to describe its features and benefits (without a PowerPoint presentation).

- Listen more and talk less.

- Visit the customer's website before the meeting to look for a message from the director of the library, new initiatives, revenue forecasts, and so on.

- Respect the librarian's time and keep the meeting to an hour or less.

It's no coincidence that the checklists for the information professional and the salesperson are remarkably similar. There is a duality of purpose for both parties: to provide a product that is appropriate for the library.

Preparing for a Sales Meeting

In sports, coaches go over the game films of their teams' opponents to create a plan that draws on the team's strengths and takes advantage of the opposition's weaknesses. Bleary-eyed coaches spend countless hours in the film room looking for a flaw in their competition that they can exploit. Even during the actual game, adjustments are made when a team uncovers a weakness in their opponent. Sales meeting preparation is not as intense as a sports rivalry, but it needs to be as complete as any coach's work to prepare the team for the next game.

Sales management's role is not only to hire talented, knowledgeable, and experienced salespeople but also to train them to follow the company's methodology. Management should prepare the sales staff for the many meetings they will inevitably have during the course of the selling year. In most organizations dealing with the library market, the sales staff has renewal goals for their current base business, which is referred to as their "book." Sales reps are also are tasked with new business goals, which involve additional products to be sold, whether to new or existing customers.

Given that there are renewal goals and new business goals, a sales rep has to be well organized to understand the features and benefits of all the products to be sold and to make the appropriate number of sales calls in the territory. At the end of the year, reps are judged by how much they "grew" the business from the previous year. Too much time spent chasing renewals can be detrimental to finding new business opportunities, and exceeding one's goals in new business can sadly be washed away by lack of success in renewals. Thus, it is incumbent upon reps to divide their time successfully between new and renew so that the expectations for both are met.

In running this financial and timing gauntlet, the sales rep must continually make phone calls to arrange meetings, prospect for new clients, and be the liaison between the customer and the sales company's home office. The rep must also make the most of those one-hour meetings at each library so as to make sure all topics are completely covered and the information professional has all the facts at hand to make a purchase.

Librarians, while not saddled with renewal and new business goals, have other time priorities they must manage. For virtually every database product on the market, there are a number of competitors vying for the librarian's attention. Most likely, those salespeople have also done their prospecting homework and know that their product is probably a viable one for the library. Perhaps they know the librarian through the Special Libraries Association (SLA) and American Library Association (ALA) directories, LinkedIn, blogs, Twitter, or personal contact at previous meetings. They *all* will call, and they *all* will want to make an appointment, and, believe me, they *all* will come knocking on the librarian's door. Therefore, as part of the librarian's daily routine, time needs to be set aside to meet and greet the sales reps. It's the rep's job to call on the library, and it's the info pro's role to meet and greet those salespeople. Librarians in "avoidance" mode—meaning they deflect as many sales meeting requests as possible—are ultimately doing a disservice to their organization. The salesperson is there to present new products and new technologies, all of which will improve the library's holdings.

Whether a database covers humanities, social science, business, music, or some other topic, for every product there will be three or four competitors, which means information professionals can expect three or four sales calls for every one subject-related database. To be anything but prepared for those encounters will spell doom for the librarian.

Whether conducted by phone, WebEx or Skype, or in person, any meeting has its own set of challenges. When the information professional is prepared, knows the rationale for the meeting, and has more than a cursory understanding of the product to be presented, then both parties can resolve the issues at hand.

Different Meetings for Different Purposes

There are a number of different kinds of sales meetings. Among them are meetings to get acquainted with each other, to discuss a renewal and thus retain existing business, or to explore new needs and possible solutions. Then there is the salesperson's favorite: the closing meeting. All of those meetings have their place, and all are part of the process of buying and selling.

Each of the types of meetings that I'll cover here has a specific purpose:

1. Initial introduction meeting. This meeting is the first time the rep and the librarian are conferring, and it is usually conducted over the phone. The rep needs to find out what the librarian's information needs are to determine whether the company has an appropriate product to fill those needs. Once a possible need has been established, then a face-to-face meeting can be scheduled. Any discussion of pricing should be avoided at this early stage.

2. On-site discovery meeting. With common ground established in the introductory phone meeting, during the longer face-to-face meeting that follows, the rep will go through a series of more specific questions to elicit a clearer definition of the library's information needs. There may or may not be a demo of the proposed product at this meeting, and price should not be discussed unless the librarian has a clear mandate to buy the product with a specified budget that has to be spent by a certain date. This meeting, if successful, will lead the way to more discussions on trial use, training, and technology assessment.

3. Meeting at a trade show for further discovery. Sometimes, the librarian and sales rep may agree to meet at the next association trade show on neutral ground. This is an excellent place for information professionals to get an in-depth demo by highly qualified product experts of the databases they are considering for purchase. The trade show is also a good place for the rep to introduce the customer to senior sales and marketing management, training staff, and other key executives of the company. At the same time, the information professional has the opportunity to see products from a variety of vendors, so as to make a well-educated choice among the various options.

4. Renewal and retention meeting. Renewing subscriptions is an integral part of a salesperson's responsibilities in the information industry. A meeting to renew current subscriptions for another year also provides an opportune time to "upsell" or "upgrade" the current coverage to include more products and services. Many times, database providers will offer special discounts to current customers as an incentive to upgrade to more content.

Database providers derive a significant amount of their revenue from renewal business. This is analogous to annuities in the insurance business. At the renewal meeting, the information professional needs to be keenly aware that these discussions with the rep provide excellent opportunities to negotiate a better deal on their price going forward. An information professional does not have to accept the initial renewal price as presented and should use this time to explore possible alternative pricing considerations. Don't expect retroactive price discounts. Any discussion at this point about discounts relates to subscriptions going forward. Unless it's a complex deal involving years forward and historical, price discounts usually are not granted for past purchases.

5. *Closing meeting.* This is the culmination of all previous meetings. All questions thus far have been answered. Demos have been performed to show the salient points of the electronic resources, technical services, or database product in question. This is the only meeting where a substantive discussion of price should take place.

Leverage and Momentum

When a salesperson calls to make an appointment, the leverage and momentum is on the side of the rep. The salesperson has determined through diligent research that the library is a prime prospect for a particular product. The rep then calls to make an appointment with the librarian, prepares for the meeting, arrives with information in hand, and makes a case for the library to consider buying the product presented.

Interestingly, after that first face-to-face meeting, the information professional holds the upper hand in every subsequent meeting. This is because once a product has been identified that fits a specific need of the library, the momentum of the negotiation shifts to the library representative. The librarian knows that if vendor A can't come to terms on price, technology, or any of a host of other issues, then vendor B will be waiting in the wings, likely with a competitive product at an attractive price. Perhaps the librarian doesn't like to deal with vendor B because of past experience. If she mentions this to vendor A, he may be motivated to fulfill all the library's demands in order to get her business in other areas. Many vendors are vying for the information professional's business, giving the latter an enormous advantage in the negotiation process.

If it's a renewal, the leverage is even more in favor of the library. If a renewal has gone up 5 percent over last year, the vendor will seriously consider a counteroffer and usually will not walk away from the renewal if the library offers to renew at 1 percent or 2 percent.

Negotiating Price

In virtually all of the sessions I have conducted for librarians about negotiation skills, the topic of price is always discussed. Many people are uncomfortable talking about price, be it in their personal lives or their professional lives. It's the 800-pound gorilla in the room. But the fact is that if you are buying information, you need to know how the vendor arrived at the price.

The first thing I'm typically asked is when the topic of price should come up in meetings with salespeople. My advice is for the information professional to wait until all aspects of the deal are clear. The info pro should never volunteer even a ballpark price unless there is complete satisfaction with all the elements of the product presented, a full examination of competing products has been performed, and there is full awareness of the budget allocated and in what time period that money needs to be spent by the library.

Following these guidelines, price is usually discussed in the last meeting, which is what makes that meeting the most important. It all comes down to a serious give-and-take between the library and the sales rep about finances. And the question under consideration is, *What is the bottom line for both parties?*

In other words, *How much does the library have to spend, and how much will the company sell its products for?*

The discussion of what the resource will cost involves four considerations:

1. The price offered is in line with similar products produced by other vendors.

2. The price falls within the budgetary guidelines set by the library administration.

3. The product being considered is the best available on the market today.

4. This database will fit in well with the other collections in this category at the library.

If all four of these elements are acceptable and the two parties have moved to the closing meeting, the information professional now moves into the most powerful position in the buying process. The librarian is in control of the next step—because the rep knows the product is well suited to the library, knows the approximate budget that has been allocated, and knows that the librarian wants to buy it. The rep also knows that now is the time when the librarian can use leverage to attempt to "sweeten the deal."

As a purchaser, the information professional has a number of possible options to throw on the table at this juncture. For example:

- If I authorize the order form today, are there any special billing considerations that you can apply to this order? I want to pay half now and the other half in 6 months.

- I would like a 3-month free trial period tacked on to the beginning (or end) of this subscription year, effectively giving me 15 months of access for the price of 12.

- If I give you a multiyear commitment, can you reduce the price by 20 percent (or more)?

- On a multiyear commitment, what additional discount can you give me if I pay the full cost of all the years up front?

- If I have any technical difficulties accessing the data throughout the life of the subscription, what is my recourse? Can I void the agreement? If so, are there cancellation penalties? Do I get my money back?

- My colleague at another library that purchased this database from your company told me about a special deal they received. Can you do the same for me?

Every one of these inquiries and concerns is legitimate. The salesperson may not have the authority to agree to all of the requests, but at the very least, he will take all the information professional's inquiries back to the office for internal discussion.

At this point, the librarian can also walk away if she is not receiving what she perceives to be fair value and honest negotiations from the sales rep. There are alternatives. If you don't ask, you will not receive.

Here is something else for the information professional to keep in mind: If it's the end of the month and the sales team has not met its sales goals, the librarian may find that all the requests for discount considerations are granted. There are some VPs of sales whose strength of resolve in granting discounts is based on each individual month's attainment of the total sales target. If the sales team is far below target that month, the sale to your library may be the one that puts the team over the top. I'm not saying this happens often, but it does happen. Conversely, if the team is having a blowout month, the chance of getting significant discounts approved by the boss greatly diminishes.

Librarians also have negotiation power when it comes to renewals, as shown in this example:

"Phil, I notice that you have included a 5 percent increase in our renewal price over last year," the librarian may say.

"That's right, Alice. We have added a significant amount of content to that database, and, of course, our costs are rising," the rep may reply.

"I appreciate that Phil, but I am under severe financial constraints at the library, which allows me to pay a maximum increase of only 2.5 percent. And after all, the inflation rate increase is well below the 5 percent you guys are charging. I cannot pay more than 2.5 percent over last year and hopefully less than that."

What happened here?

The librarian is practicing the age-old tradition of negotiation. Many times a vendor will consider flexibility in the rate of increase on their renewals. The astute information professional will use that knowledge to negotiate a more palatable price increase over the previous years' rate. It might even be possible to negotiate a price reduction.

It is highly unlikely that the sales rep will walk away from a valued customer for a few percentage points on the renewal. The information professional has significant leverage and, when possible, should judiciously use that power.

Throughout the price negotiations, the information professional has every right to ask a vendor to defend its price and to ask what specific developments are needed to improve the offering, and at the very least should ask to see the vendor's price sheet. The bottom line is that the librarian has an enormous amount of power at virtually every point in the process, especially in hard economic times when orders from new customers are not coming in as swiftly as companies would like. Moreover, in tough times renewal rates often take a plunge as well. Salespeople are taught to "ask for the order." Information professionals should abide by the same principle. Ask for whatever you feel will make the purchase more palatable for the library. Because, in the end, the worst that can happen is that the vendor says "no." On the other hand, you may be pleasantly surprised when they say "yes."

Using an Agenda

One of the most crucial aspects of the buying and selling process is making sure that the salesperson and the information professional are on the same path, traveling to a mutually acceptable destination. Many a sale has been lost because the salesperson and the client had totally different views of the outcome of their meeting.

Each party has various *objectives* tied to specific *outcomes*. The salesperson wants to sell a product. When the sale is made, the customer is satisfied and the rep makes a commission for the sale, getting closer to the yearly sales goal.

The objective for the information professional is to acquire quality products at a reasonable price that are a good fit for the library's collections. In the case of a university library, for example, the outcome will be that it will have the necessary resources to support research and attract premier students and a more distinguished faculty.

In my consulting practice, whenever I have the opportunity to work with information professionals, the question of the use of an agenda prior to an important meeting always meets with the same response. At a recent SLA meeting, I spoke to a group of librarians from corporate, legal, and academic libraries, and asked the following: "By a show of hands, how many of you require the salesperson to provide an agenda of the items to be discussed at your upcoming meeting? And let me qualify that question so that we all understand that I am asking only in relation to important meetings."

Only one person raised her hand in the affirmative, and she later admitted that she really didn't use the agenda as much as she would like. If an information professional comes away with one solid "to do" item from reading this book, I hope that will be to demand that a sales rep coming in for a substantive meeting provide an agenda prior to the meeting.

By the way, later in the afternoon I ran into the lady from my session who had sheepishly raised her hand when I asked the agenda question:

> "Mike, I am so glad you reinforced the agenda issue. I called my boss after your suggestion and we are now putting into practice a policy of asking for an agenda from vendors prior to substantive meetings," she said.

By delineating the topics for discussion in advance of the meeting, the rep and the librarian immediately start walking down the same road together. Maybe initially not arm-in-arm, but at least they are starting out on the same path.

Salespeople are much like the librarians in that SLA class, and I am often surprised that so few of them take the time to send an agenda to their clients/prospects prior to a scheduled meeting, especially since it's such a simple concept. The most successful salespeople I have worked with are those who employ an agenda as part of their normal preparation and selling process.

The agenda, usually sent out a week before the meeting, should describe the topics to be discussed and who is planning to attend the meeting. For example, the librarian may say that the director of the library has been invited to next week's meeting. The fact that the customer wants to bring the boss into the meeting signals a serious interest in the product and indicates to the sales rep that perhaps a senior sales executive should attend from that side as well. Having people of similar stature within their respective organizations at the meeting puts both parties on equal footing. Furthermore, the two senior executives probably have the power to directly negotiate price and make buying decisions.

Today more than at any previous time in our economic history, the expression "time is money" is not only applicable— it's the very cornerstone of how we conduct our business affairs. Customers no longer have the luxury of having extended meetings with salespeople. They simply do not have the time, and even if they did, their management would frown on the practice.

My first year in sales was rocky, to say the least. I came to the job with no experience. Prior to being hired as a sales rep, I had been a schoolteacher and played saxophone in a band. Every day as a salesperson in the corporate world was a learning experience for me. I had been hired along with another guy whose experience in selling was on the same level as mine. We would arrive at work each day, exchange pleasantries, and wonder how we both got involved in this odd endeavor. Success was not certain for either of us, as door after library door was slammed in our faces.

One day, my boss approached me and asked if I could help my colleague become more successful in making appointments over the phone. Apparently, he was having great difficulty getting the appointments. The first call we made together was to a great prospect for him in Manhattan. We both felt that if we could get in to see this librarian, we could make a presentation that would result in a sale.

I made the call to the prospect on my colleague's behalf, introduced myself, and gave my 30-second elevator speech. Unfortunately the prospect responded by telling me, in no uncertain terms, that he did not like our product, had no need for the product, and didn't want to hear from me or the other guy who called him earlier in the week ever again. This was quite distressing since I knew our product was a perfect fit for this particular library. Although initially disappointed, we were determined not to give up and tried to devise a strategy that, at the very least, would give us an audience with the librarian.

Since it was clear that calling again was not a viable option, we decided to send the prospect an email to once again introduce the company and the two of us. We briefly told him how we could be of service and then proceeded to list agenda items for his approval, for a meeting to be scheduled and held at his convenience. Furthermore, we encouraged him to add to the agenda or delete any of the proposed items, and we listed both our phone numbers just in case he actually wanted to speak to either of us.

A few days later, I received a phone call from the librarian telling me that he was willing to see us. He was specific with the time and date and made sure to inform me that the time slot he allocated for our meeting was limited in length and that we had better not waste his time. We confirmed the date and time, along with the topics to be discussed. Just as he was about to hang up, he thanked us for the agenda and lamented that most sales reps did not give him the courtesy we had extended. Sending the agenda indicated a respect for his time, which resulted in his granting us the meeting. It's all about mutual respect.

We arrived at the library at the appointed time and date. While I know we made a great presentation, we did not get the order that day. Eventually the other sales rep left the company, and I inherited the account. I am proud to say this librarian eventually became a customer. What's more, he and I developed a long-standing friendship that lasted up until his retirement many years later.

As a result of this encounter, I began to include an agenda with many of my sales appointments, and I encouraged the customer to add and delete any topics. Composing the agenda took no more than 10 minutes of my time, and those few minutes added tens of thousands of dollars to my earnings. I'd say that agreeing on an agenda in advance of your meeting is time well spent for the librarian and the salesperson.

W.I.I.F.M. (What's In It For Me)

W.I.I.F.M. is the universal radio station heard all over the world without commercial interruption. Customers are always asking, "How will the product or service you're trying to sell help me personally and how will it help my organization?" Notice that the "me" took precedence over the "organization," hence the question, *What's in it for me?*

Every time a salesperson visits, the customer is thinking, consciously or subconsciously, "How will the purchase of this person's product/service benefit me? Will it make me a hero in the eyes of my boss? Will having the product save me time and money? Will it get those pesky people on the third floor the information they've been unable to obtain by themselves? Is it relevant to our needs at the library? Does this vendor have a competitor that has a better product?"

In baseball, a batter is deemed extraordinary if his batting average is above 300. A 300 batting average means that the player has gotten a hit 3 out of 10 times at bat. That also means that he did not get a hit 7 of the 10 times. The batter failed 70 percent of the time, and yet that 300 average in baseball means he's a very good and highly regarded hitter. A salesperson who experiences success in 1 out of 10 visits is just as extraordinary as the 300 batter on the baseball diamond. It's all relative. Rejection is part of the job. The reality is that a salesperson's efforts are rejected most of the time.

Sales is not a career for the weak. Salespeople constantly hear about declining budgets or no one being available to approve the purchase. The most common comments salesmen hear to signal the non-sale are "I'll let you know" or "I'll call you next week."

Each day, salespeople all over the world do their prospecting, follow up on their pending proposals, prepare for their sales meetings, get dressed up, travel to their appointments, and make their presentations. Yet, when they leave the prospect's office, most of the time they are no better off than they were before they started the process. In many cases the problem is that the rep has failed to recognize—and embrace the knowledge—that their prospect was tuning in to W.I.I.F.M.

The majority of library people I have met over my career are basically very nice. As a result, they tend to try and let salespeople down easy when they know the sale won't happen. One reason for a rep to send an agenda in advance of the meeting is to ascertain a realistic level of interest. Second, structuring the sales meeting as a probing exercise helps the rep become more efficient in determining whether the prospect is truly interested. If the prospect is interested, does the institution have the necessary funds for purchase? Finally, the rep needs to understand the most important principle in the decision-making process: W.I.I.F.M. What will the purchase of a database do for the prospect on both the personal and business level? What will the possible purchase of electronic resources do for the prospect's boss? In other words, what's in it for all of them if they make a buying decision?

Wise salespeople know that part of their job is to make sure that the product being presented makes sense to the prospect on any number of levels:

> "Mr. Prospect, you have indicated that you need a more reliable way to predict fiduciary outcomes for the company's internal travel database. If I can provide a product that gives you that data quickly and efficiently and provides reliable, accurate results, would that be a positive outcome?"
>
> "Yes, that would be an excellent outcome for me, my department, and my manager."

To find out how all parties will profit, the rep should move the conversation from benefits to the library to possible career benefits for the prospects:

"How will the purchase of the product help you personally on a daily basis?"

"My boss has been all over me for this data. If your program really delivers accurate and timely data, I will be a hero to that lady in the corner office."

Bingo! The rep has uncovered a personal pain point of his prospect. The boss's need for this data has been a millstone around the neck of the intended customer. The rep will now help the prospect become the hero he wants to be and make the pain go away. If he's a hero, the boss is happy, and after all, don't we *all* want our bosses to be happy?

For sales reps, being aware of W.I.I.F.M. is a major point toward achieving success. It doesn't matter what is being sold. In the end—no matter the cost, the complexity of the product, or the people in the conversation—every customer wants the same thing: to gain professional success and approval from their supervisors, staff, or peers. A good salesperson understands this concept and does everything possible to make the prospect look great within her own organization.

Visualizing the Sales Meeting

We would all like to be able to predict the future, read tea leaves, or buy that elusive stock that will quadruple in value overnight. If such powers existed, casinos in Las Vegas would have to close their doors because everyone would be cashing in giant stacks of chips. Fortunately for casino operators, most people don't have those abilities. (Some people think they do, but that's another issue.)

In sales, the best any rep can do in predicting a sale is to be well prepared for discussions with the client. Understanding the prospect, knowing how the library has done business in the past, and being aware of an information professional's history with certain companies all serve to create a base of information that the astute rep can apply.

Understanding in advance what may happen during the sales meeting requires intuitive skills that become honed after many years of attending countless sales meetings. Even sales reps with many years of service can become a bit nervous when calling on certain accounts. It's not so much that they are unable to fulfill their role; it's just the way they operate. Once they are in front of the customer, everything works fine. Anticipation of the upcoming event is often worse than the event itself.

To counteract nervousness or fear of the unknown prior to a sales visit, I often advise salespeople to visualize the upcoming meeting:

> "If you say X, what do you think your prospect will say? How will they react?" I ask.
>
> "I expect severe pushback on this aspect of the product," the rep responds.
>
> "Do you think the pushback is based solely on price?" I inquire.
>
> "No, price is not the issue at that library. It comes down to a reluctance to try something new. It is a very traditional library and will never jump on the bandwagon first. It is usually the last one to bring in something like our product, waiting until other libraries have it already."
>
> "So to counteract this reluctance, you could tell them how this product is being successfully used at one of their major competitors," I respond.

The bottom line is that role playing, or just simply visualizing what may happen, gives the rep confidence and familiarity. That's not to say that every role-play uncovers every question and concern ahead of time, of course.

For me, the best tactic in visualizing the sales meeting is to ask, "What are the five worst questions the customer can ask you?" Most salespeople are pretty good at predicting what may go wrong. As head of sales, prior to a meeting I would have the reps list the expected questions, and together we would answer them so that when the rep was in front of the customer, the fear of the unknown was considerably reduced. More often than not, the worst questions we imagined would be asked never materialized, but the few that did were aptly answered.

Recently I had a conversation with a young salesperson. She asked me if, in addition to visualizing the future sales meeting, I also used a roadmap of questions as I met with customers and prospects:

> "Did you just ask questions or did you instinctively know what your prospect wanted?'
>
> "As I progressed in my career, I usually had a pretty good idea of what they needed," I said. "But I never took it for granted. I needed verification and to arrive at that, there were 10 to 15 questions I always asked."
>
> "Did you follow a script in your head as you probed for the customers' pain points?"
>
> "I always asked the same 10 to 15 questions," I told her. "And after a while, those questions were so ingrained in me, that they just came out automatically, but I always wrote down the answers. Those answers were my notes as I reviewed the responses with the librarian at the conclusion of the meeting."

The questioning was the easy part. You ask, they tell; you write down the responses, review the responses at the end of the meeting, and make the recommendation. The important part is to let the customer do the majority of the talking. A rep cannot make recommendations or review the highlights of the meeting if he was the one doing most of the speaking.

KNOWLEDGE POINTS

- Salespeople and information professionals have a vested interest in seeing each other succeed.

- At all meetings, the information professional and the salesperson should both practice the Three C's: be clear, be concise, and be current.

- An agenda provided by the sales rep and reviewed by the information professional prior to their meeting clearly delineates what will (and will not) be discussed and who else will be joining the meeting. It defines expectations and outcomes. Submitting an agenda in advance of the meeting shows respect for the customer's time and ensures that both parties are on the same track.

- The sales process involves a series of visits, phone calls, and demos.

- As the meetings move toward the final outcome, the greater advantage goes to the buyer. The librarian needs to take advantage of this fact to negotiate the best deal.

- Price should only enter into the conversation when the info pro has a clear vision of the product presented, knows the actual amount of funds to be allocated, and has identified the time frame of when monies need to be spent.

- Customers are all listening to the same radio station: W.I.I.F.M. Sales reps need to understand that, aside from the actual content being sold, customers are interested in what a product can do for them personally.

- Helping the information professional acquire appropriate products should be the salesperson's key objective.

- Visualizing the upcoming sales meeting helps both the sales rep and the information professional better prepare.

- The consultative sales approach teaches sales reps to ask a series of questions to uncover the specific needs of the customer.

- A good salesperson lets the customer do most of the speaking at the meeting.

Publisher's note: Some of this chapter was adapted from an article by Michael Gruenberg published in the March/April 2012 edition of *Information Outlook* magazine, a publication of the Special Libraries Association.

Sales = Showtime

In the song "Karn Evil 9" (written by Keith Emerson, Greg Lake, and Peter Sinfield), the band Emerson, Lake & Palmer sing: "Welcome back my friends to the show that never ends. We're so glad you could attend. Come inside! Come inside!" Much like ELP's song, the salesperson is welcoming the customer to hear what it is the rep is selling. "Showtime" is a term used by some salespeople to describe how they feel before going into a sales appointment. It translates to being positive in demeanor and authoritative about the product, and understanding that their role is to help the customer.

Being Positive Usually Brings Success

Positive attitudes empower negotiations. Self-confidence is a fundamental personality trait in every successful salesperson. Enthusiasm is infectious. A salesperson with a positive mental attitude (PMA) knows that his customers will pick up on it and become empowered by the rep's confidence. The most successful salespeople understand that, at any presentation, first they entertain and then they inform.

That inner confidence comes through in every aspect of the salesperson's daily being. Whether it's speaking on the phone, participating at a sales meeting, or just conversing with management and colleagues, PMA always come to the forefront. People with PMA energize every encounter. Others feel the vibe.

I once managed an excellent sales rep who, unfortunately, was having a less than successful social life. She would arrive at the office in a foul mood and a depressed state every Monday. Her negative mental attitude was not only affecting her sales performance; it was also having an impact on her relationships with her colleagues in the office. The other reps found it difficult to be around her, especially on a Monday morning after a long, lonely weekend. By Tuesday, she was usually over it, and as the week wore on, she got back to being a more pleasant co-worker. But the negativity reared its ugly head on too many occasions to suit me.

I was convinced that her busy travel schedule masked her ultimate desire to stay away from her apartment in the city on weekends. She traveled extensively, and, many times when out of town on business trips, she worked late into Friday and took a plane home on Saturday afternoon, thus eliminating any chance of facing her personal dilemma of no social life on the weekends.

I often reminded her that she was a person of exceptional sales talent. She had consistently hit her numbers, had good relations with most of her customers, and had been one of our top reps before she broke up with her long-standing significant other. She had the talent; she just needed to refocus her efforts and move on from the failed personal relationship. Her personal life was getting in the way of her business success.

Fortunately, she took my advice and reexamined her behavior, especially on those Monday mornings. She once again became a productive salesperson, and, with her newly regained self-confidence, she eventually met a very nice new significant other.

When we go through a personal crisis, even the best of us can lose confidence in ourselves. We may ask ourselves, *Why did this happen to me? What did I do wrong?* Mostly likely, you may never know—and, quite frankly, no one in your office really cares.

Tips for the Salesperson

The bottom line is that salespeople are paid to sell a product. You can't sell a product if you are depressed and lack confidence in yourself. That negativity comes through loud and clear. You can't appear successful to others if you don't inwardly feel successful.

Sales = Showtime. A manager may be sympathetic, but she ultimately doesn't care about your personal problems. The manager's job is to help all the reps to sell. A sales rep's job is to be enthusiastic and exude a certain confidence that will inevitably be picked up by the prospect. Whether buyers or sellers, people like to be around people that are upbeat. No one likes a complainer. In the words of one of my favorite salespeople, if you're depressed and in a sales situation, you need to "get over yourself!"

Tips for the Information Professional

While I cannot claim to have ever managed a library or library staff, I certainly know many people in the profession. Having called on virtually every type of library throughout the world, I have had the good fortune of interacting with deans of library schools, library directors, reference librarians, acquisitions librarians, and subject specialists, and so on.

For the most part, dealing with info pros has been quite rewarding, but I have noticed that some library folks have difficulty in dealing with salespeople. In some cases, the sales rep is viewed as the enemy, someone not to be trusted. I'm here to tell you that the sales rep is really your friend. The rep is the person who knows the product, knows the special deals, and is only too willing to be of service.

When the librarian keeps the rep at an arm's length, that negative attitude comes to the forefront in their interaction. To counteract that attitude, the info pro must also prepare for "showtime." Even if the librarian does not like the rep or the company—as is a person's prerogative—in the interest of obtaining the best product at the best price, the librarian should smile, ask questions, and never let the rep know she would rather be somewhere else.

Whether your profession is in sales or librarianship, if your personal life is getting in the way of success, follow this simple three-step process, and your outlook is guaranteed to improve significantly:

1. **Get serious about your job.** At the very least, your job is a good diversion from your personal problems. Get serious about your work, and, by putting some distance between your personal life and work, you'll eventually find the problems may not seem quite as dire.

2. **Get back on track.** The beautiful aspect of selling or buying information is that the basic principles of both always come down to a simple proven formula: Probing questions and answers about needs and budget, as well as careful research, will provide the solution; ergo, the sale and a satisfied customer.

3. **Get going.** Stop feeling sorry for yourself. No one relates well to a pitiful person. Negativism is the kiss of death.

And if these three steps are too much to comprehend, try this: "Fake it until you feel it."

Making a Good First Impression

Whether you sell clothing at Neiman-Marcus or home appliances at Sears, you need to always look your best. People make immediate decisions about you based on your appearance before they consciously know they have done so. A study published in *Nature Neuroscience* in 2008 revealed that unconscious decision-making is done as quickly as 10 seconds prior to realizing you have done so.

How you look, how you walk into the room, how you greet the person with whom you are meeting—that's all processed in milliseconds. Even before people consciously make a value judgment about you, their brains already have. You need to know how you come across to the other person. I always likened this part of the meeting to playing tennis. Is your appearance a strong serve, or is it a lob that barely crosses the net?

Does that tie or scarf complement that shirt? Is that color really a good one for you? Are your shoes shined? A poor choice of colors, inappropriate blouse designs, or an unconventional hairstyle immediately sets a tone that may cause the other person to think, "Why did I even allow this person to enter my office?"

The former president of a large information industry company related a story to me about a search that his company was doing to recruit a salesperson. They had interviewed a number of candidates, and, after the first round, the HR director came into the president's office and asked which candidates should be brought back for the second and decisive round of interviews.

The HR person and the president liked only three candidates of the many that had been interviewed. They were all good candidates, although the HR person was pushing very hard for one specific finalist:

> "Candidate A is very good on so many levels," the HR rep confidently said.
>
> "Yes, I liked him, too, and he has great qualifications. He has the potential to be very successful for us, but I don't want to hire him," responded the president.
>
> "Why?" she asked incredulously.
>
> "I noticed he wasn't wearing socks at the interview. He had a great suit, a nice shirt and tie, shined shoes, but no socks. I'm concerned about that," he said.

After much discussion, they decided to bring this candidate back for the final round of interviews. He got the job and promised to wear socks every day. In this case, even though the candidate's attire raised a red flag, he got the job. Why? Because everything else about him met the standards of the company. He apparently decided to show that he was cool by not wearing socks to the interview but, instead, almost blew the chance to work for the company. He got away with it because someone internally vouched for his talent and he got a second chance.

You don't get a second chance when you walk in the door or you greet someone from behind a desk for the first time, so it is best to always look your best. Before you leave home, realistically assess how you look; if you don't like the way you look, change your outfit. If you see a flaw or two in what you are wearing, imagine what others will see.

In his brilliant book, *Frank's Rules: How to Sell Menswear (and Practically Anything Else) Extremely Well* (AuthorHouse, 2009), Frank Schipani talks about dressing for success. He relates a story about Arnold Rothstein, a notorious gambler, gangster, and powerful leader of the Jewish mafia in New York in the 1920s. Rothstein mentored two up-and-coming gangsters, Lucky Luciano and Meyer Lansky, on how they needed to dress for success. He pointed out that they could not expect to influence politicians, business leaders, and other gangsters if they dressed like street thugs. Rothstein, Luciano, and Lansky learned their lessons well. They set the tone of being well dressed for many future gangland criminals. You don't have to be in the crime business to know that a well dressed person exudes an aura of confidence. When a salesperson calls on a customer, or a prospective client appears at his office, the way he is dressed sets the tone for the meeting.

When I started as a schoolteacher in New York City in the late 1960s, I realized that dress codes for teachers were eliminated. I had expected to see my teaching colleagues dressing the way I remembered my teachers when I was a high school student in New York. But I was surprised to see a number of them arriving each day in jeans and t-shirts. Maybe I was clinging to old standards and beliefs, but that ultra-casual style was not the example I wanted to set for the students. The first step in gaining the respect of your audience is to be respectful of your audience. How could I impart the knowledge that I was supposed give to these kids if I looked like one of their pals from the neighborhood?

I knew I had to buy new business clothes, since after a few years in college, my business wardrobe was virtually non-existent. Salary for a beginning teacher at that time was relatively low, but nevertheless I went out and bought three new suits, two new sports jackets, and a number of ties and shirts so I could at least look professional for my new teaching job. I felt that as an educator, I needed to differentiate myself from the students. After all, they were looking to me as a leader and a person of intelligence. If I dressed like the kids, how would they respect me and ultimately learn their lessons?

Fortunately, many of the other young teachers who began teaching with me that fall felt the same as I did. One particular teacher and I gave each other hints on style and shared locations of men's stores. It would be fair to say that we had a friendly competition on who looked the best wearing the latest styles.

I had the great pleasure to know the late Mortimer Levitt, who was the founder of the Custom Shirt shops. Levitt had an extraordinary eye for men's fashion and wrote several how-to books on the subject: *The Executive Look: How to Get It, How to Keep It* (Atheneum, 1981) and *Class: What It Is and How to Acquire It* (Atheneum, 1984). In those books, he gives valuable pointers to people of all sizes on how to dress appropriately.

Books on the topic of dressing for success, like Schipani's and Levitt's, need to be part of a professional library, along with the other titles that help you to advance in your chosen profession.

KNOWLEDGE POINTS

- Sales = Showtime. A good salesperson knows that we all are simply players acting in a real-life melodrama. Demonstrate confidence, poise, and polish whenever you are in front of your audience and give them the best show on earth.

- If you have a job that deals with the public, remember, you are on stage. If that makes you uncomfortable, find a job in the library that doesn't deal with people.

- Personal problems need to be left at home and not brought into the office.

- Enthusiasm is easily communicated by phone and certainly apparent at face-to-face meetings. Conversely, lack of enthusiasm is even more noticeable.

- What you wear speaks volumes about you before you open your mouth.

Time Management: Mr. and Ms. Clock

"Time is on my side, yes it is" sang The Rolling Stones (written by Jerry Ragavoy) on their *12 X 5* album. Time may have been on their side, but it's not on anyone's side if that time is being wasted with extraneous exercises.

What about communication is different today than it was 100 years ago? Most people will say that there was no internet 100 years ago, while today we can communicate instantaneously with one another via email, texting, IM, and other electronic means. Other people may note that, because of worldwide news coverage, we can witness a revolution in any part of the world as it happens. We don't have to wait until the next day to learn about events in the morning newspaper.

Today, we have high-speed printing presses, YouTube, and streaming videos. We have iPads, iPods, and downloadable music that sounds great through our mini earphones. We have smartphones that allow us not only to communicate but also to play video games, pay bills, and watch the latest exploits of our sports heroes. We had none of that even 25 years ago.

OK, so we know what is different. But what about communication is the *same* today as it was 100 years ago? That answer is very simple: There are still only 24 hours in a day, and there will still be only 24 hours in a day 100 years from now. That being said, the way we manage our time is even more crucial today than it was 100 years ago. We have more distractions today that can take us away from our day-to-day responsibilities. It's hard to keep focus when so many diversions are vying for our attention.

Managing Time as a Salesperson

My first sales manager used to say that an hour wasted today is an hour that will never come back tomorrow. He was absolutely correct. That's why the efficient use of time is one of the most important aspects of the salesperson's job. Poor time management will kill a career every time.

In sales, a rep has to make calls with a better than average chance of reaching the customer. The time period to best call and reach the other person is referred to as "prime time." Prime time is crucial, and anything other than direct sales activities during this time is a waste for a sales rep.

Salespeople have only approximately 80 hours a month of "prime time" for selling at their disposal. That's 80 hours to sell, renew, visit, and make quota. Those 80 hours translate into 4 hours a day or 20 hours a week. If sales reps do not use those prime hours to sell, they will probably not be successful. Let's break down those hours and see why there are only limited amounts of time for sales activities.

Most customers usually arrive at work somewhere before 9 AM. They say hello to their colleagues, review what was on television the night before, prepare a cup of coffee or tea, and get ready for the day. That means that they will settle in to work somewhere around 9:30 to 9:45 AM. To avoid getting the dreaded voice message that the customer is unavailable, the best time to call a prospect or customer is from 10 AM to noon.

Somewhere around noon, these same people are getting ready for lunch. Lunch hour for many of us also involves chores and errands—a visit to a local store or a quick trip to the kids' school for a meeting with the teacher.

Assuming most employees are back at work sometime before 2 PM, another good time to call is between 2 and 4 PM. After 4 PM is probably a little too late to call because people are now thinking about picking up their kids from afterschool care, deciding on something for dinner, or putting finishing touches on a report that's due in the morning. For a salesperson to work effectively, the knowledge and use of prime time for selling is crucial.

What about those times in the day outside of prime time? How should the rep use that time effectively? There are many other things that successful salespeople can do with their non-prime time hours to ensure that their prime time hours are as productive as possible. During non-prime times, a salesperson can:

- **Work on expense reports.** Expense reports should never be filled out during prime time. Complete them early in the morning, late in the afternoon, or early at night.

- **Organize a call list.** Compile the list of planned calls for the next day so that time is not wasted looking up numbers or deciding whom to call during prime time.

- **Devise a schedule for each day.** For example, the salesperson may want to spend from 10 to 11 AM making new business calls and from 11 AM to noon making follow-up calls from last weeks' appointments. No matter how the rep decides to structure the day, he should keep to the schedule as closely as possible.

- **Make personal calls.** Calls to friends and relatives— unless they are prospects to buy your products—should be made during non-prime time hours.

- **Prospect.** There are publications, industry journals, local newspapers, and electronic news sources that are filled with names of prospects. Reading any one of these publications at lunchtime can provide new sales prospects, and one new sale a month from this activity may make the difference in meeting or exceeding sales quotas.

- **Catch up on email.** During non-prime time a rep can catch up on company emails, product news, and competitor research, and can practice sales presentations and demos.

Managing Time as an Information Professional

Do info pros work under the same "prime time" principle as sales reps?

The basics of time management also apply to information professionals. For library folks, time is also a precious commodity—so many chores with so little time to complete them all.

There are specific assignments at the reference desk. There are research projects to be done, classes to be planned and taught, and, of course, staff meetings to attend. All of this means that an info pro has a very busy day, no matter what type of library she works in. If that time is not managed properly, the results will not be productive.

For sales reps and librarians to achieve mutual success, the librarian has to devote a certain amount of time during the week to speaking with salespeople.

The senior sales rep from one of my consulting clients was visiting Washington, DC, and since I live in the area, we decided to make some calls on local prospective clients. We emailed a particular prospect who had previously expressed interest in our product to tell him the dates and times we would be available. We got no response. As the date approached, we both called this prospect and left messages regarding when we would visit the library and asking for a convenient time to meet. Again, no response. On the day we had selected, we decided to go to the library since the prospect clearly knew that we were in town and looking for an opportunity to get together.

We entered the library and told the person at the front desk that we were here to see the person we had contacted.

"Sure, let me tell him you have arrived," he said.

After a short call, the young man at the desk informed us that the person we had hoped to see did not have office hours that particular day and would be unable to see us.

Now, I'm not questioning that the person we wanted to see was busy, but he clearly knew my associate was coming to the library from another city and, at the very least, could have come out of his office, greeted us, and said that he was extremely busy and that hopefully we could meet in the not too distant future. After all, this was not an unexpected visit; we didn't just drop in. Both of us gave ample notice, and, at any time in the weeks before our visit, the librarian could have called or emailed to tell us not to come. Silence on the part of the librarian was not an option.

Information professionals must make time to meet salespeople. Some library people I know set aside a specific time each day to speak with salespeople. They understand that the sales rep who calls to make an appointment is only doing his job. It is better for the info pro to take the initiative and suggest a time for an appointment, rather than continually get voice messages from the rep. If the info pro dictates the terms and time of the initial meeting, that stance of authority will prevail throughout the entire sales process.

At the meeting, it is the information professional's responsibility to keep the rep on track, in relation to time and product description, if the rep strays off course:

> "Hey Chris, you've spent the last 20 minutes talking about your family's trip to Yellowstone. And while I love to hear about your kids, I need to know about your company's latest product. I only have 40 minutes

to give to this meeting, and we haven't even touched the surface of why you're here."

The information professional has every right and, I say, the ultimate responsibility to keep the meeting focused. Because otherwise, at the end of the meeting the rep goes home and the librarian is stuck without the information, and that benefits no one.

In summary, the info pro needs to:

- Devise a schedule that allows for time to meet with salespeople. Create that schedule well in advance. For example a 3-week view or even 1-month view gives everyone time to prepare.

- Schedule meetings in rooms that have privacy and that can accommodate more than just you and the salesperson.

- Always ask for an agenda at least 1 to 2 weeks in advance of your meeting.

- If the salesperson is not answering your questions to your satisfaction, ask for clarification. You want to leave the meeting with a clear picture of the product, its cost, and any possible sales incentives the rep can offer.

- If you simply cannot meet with the rep, let them know. Silence and avoidance is not acceptable.

Mr. and Ms. Clock

To drive home the message of time management to sales teams I managed, I created "Mr. Clock"—and later Ms. Clock—as symbols of effective time management. It was fun, we laughed a lot about it, and it reminded people how valuable a resource time can be when used properly.

If we were about to go to a trade show, our pre-show meeting would inevitably begin with "Mr. and Ms. Clock go to a trade

Figure 7.1   Mr. and Ms. Clock

show." It was humorous way to drive home the point that time at the show should be used in a productive manner. Mr. and Ms. Clock made many appearances at my sales meetings (Figure 7.1).

To make the exercise of buying and selling information efficient and successful, salespeople and librarians should place a clock on their desk as a reminder of their schedule. Even if you simply use the clock on your computer, the important point is to look at the clock and use it to guide your activities. It's all about knowing the time and using it to your best advantage.

By using a clock, a salesperson or info pro can visually track the time being spent on whatever projects are to be completed that day. Guiding yourself by the clock creates efficiency and a logical order to the day. Each person is different and will arrange each day according to his or her individual needs, but a person who plans the day in advance will be far more efficient than a person who reacts to whatever happens.

KNOWLEDGE POINTS

- Time can be your best friend or your worst enemy. Let Mr. (or Ms.) Clock guide you; then you will be operating at peak efficiency.

- "Prime time" for sales reps is for selling, and nothing else should interfere with that mission.

- Sales reps and information professionals need to organize their daily activities before the workday begins.

- Manage your time effectively by placing a clock on your desk and keeping to your own personal schedule.

- A sales rep's responsibility in the information industry is to meet with librarians. The librarian's responsibility is to meet with sales reps as a means to providing the best information to library patrons.

What a Typical Sales Meeting Looks Like

In "The Word," written by Lennon and McCartney, the Beatles sing: "Say the word and you'll be free. Say the word and be like me. Say the word I'm thinking of." At a sales meeting, the word the rep is thinking about may not be the same one the customer is thinking about. Words can flow in many different directions unless attention is paid to the structure of the meeting.

Before the Sales Meeting Begins

In expectation of the sales meeting, information professionals and sales reps should think about what they expect to learn from the other party. Both the rep and the info pro need to come to the meeting prepared to do business with one another. Both should have goals and objectives in mind before they ever sit across the table from one another. At this initial meeting, the rep is going to probe to see if the product she thinks could be applicable actually is. The information professional should approach the meeting in a similar manner—to find out if that product that piqued his interest can fit the needs of the library. In essence, they are both attending the meeting for the same purpose. It's a discovery meeting. Without an assessment of the cold hard facts each person can gain as a result of this meeting, nothing can be bought or sold.

So how do the rep and the info pro get the data they need to make the all-important assessment? Each must come to the meeting prepared with a specific set of questions to ask the other. By carefully reviewing the answers to those questions, each can decide what the next steps should be.

Here are some questions for info pros to think about prior to meeting with salespeople:

1. Are you in avoidance mode when a salesperson calls? If so, you need to change that stance since it does no one any good. Be open to the possibilities.

2. How proactive are you in understanding the current mix of new products available on the market today? (Your organization expects you to know the "latest and greatest.")

3. Have you reviewed any improvements to the products made by this vendor?

4. Do you have the negotiation skills to get the best value from the product *and* the salesperson?

5. Do you view the salesperson as an enemy or an ally? Which relationship will benefit you the most?

6. How can the salesperson help you in analyzing and understanding your costs?

7. Have you developed advocates within your organization?

8. Are you prepared with the pertinent questions for your meeting?

Aside from asking questions related to content, the info pro should be constantly assessing the rep:

1. Does your salesperson fully understand the product being presented to you? In other words, do you feel comfortable that this person really knows the product he is presenting to you and its relevance to the library's mission?

2. Can you clearly inform the rep about the buying procedures of your organization?

3. Did the salesperson send an agenda to you at least one week in advance of the meeting? If so, was it to your satisfaction? Did you not receive an agenda despite having asked for one?

On the other side of the table, the salesperson can use his own set of questions to make the meeting productive:

1. What is the objective of the meeting? Renewal, new business, strategy, a specific problem?

2. Was an agenda sent in advance of the meeting, including topics to be covered?

3. What are the anticipated key questions I can expect from the client, and how will those questions be answered? Or, put in a less delicate manner, what are the five worst questions that this librarian can ask me?

4. Did I consult with the appropriate product manager prior to the meeting, and does that person need to be at the meeting too?

5. What is the buying cycle of the client? If a new product is presented at the meeting and the client ostensibly likes it, how long will it take for the order to be signed? Are there other decision-makers that need to be contacted at this time? What is the buying process?

6. Are there other opportunities for more of our company's products at this institution? Have I researched the institution's website for that information?

7. Are there any significant events at the institution that may impact new sales or renewal?

8. If this is a large institution, how many appointments will there be that day in addition to the librarian, and with whom?

9. What is the closing strategy for this meeting?

10. Are there any technical support issues?

11. What are the next steps?

Structure of a Sales Meeting

If the sales meeting is properly managed by the sales rep, a typical meeting—if there is such a thing—should usually take an hour or less (unless the librarian and the rep are engaged in high-level negotiations) and is divided into four separate parts:

1. Introductions (10 minutes)

2. Fact-finding (30 minutes)

3. Review and Demonstrations (10 minutes): Here is the point in the sales meeting where the rep summarizes all answers, which are then confirmed by the customer. There is the possibility of a brief demo.

4. Wrap-up (5 minutes): The meeting should end with both parties going over their individual to-do lists and making plans for the next meeting.

Introductions

Introductions make up the first 5 to 10 minutes. If it is the first time the rep and librarian are meeting, then some type of introductory conversation is required. Maybe it's a word of thanks from the rep to acknowledge the librarian's efforts to make time for the meeting. Maybe it's a few words about a colleague of the librarian who suggested the meeting take place. Or maybe it's just a discussion about the weather. No matter what the topic, it's good to start with a conversation that is not business oriented as you both settle in. People doing business need to feel comfortable with one another before products, terms, and costs are ever brought to the table.

Some reps feel the need to get right into the meeting objectives without any small talk. I have always cautioned against this approach because it means both the rep and the information professional miss the opportunity to get to know one another. Unless the rep's sole purpose is to "make a sale and run," not understanding the likes and dislikes of a potential customer is dangerous and short-sighted. All the sales organizations that I have been affiliated with encourage their salespeople to develop a close working relationship with their customers. They can do that by showing interest in their customers. Databases, and related technical and legal issues, will obviously be discussed later at the meeting, so the rep should try to understand the person with whom he is speaking at the outset of the meeting.

Since sales is a job that attracts gregarious people, some sales reps may take this introductory phase a bit too literally. Sales reps can certainly talk about their summer vacation in the Napa Valley but needn't relive their experiences at every vineyard that offered a wine tasting. The information professional should steer the conversation away from nonbusiness issues if the rep seems intent on using the entire time for small talk.

Fact-Finding

The second part of the meeting is fact-finding, which should occupy the majority of the time, approximately 20 to 30 minutes. The rep should develop 10 to 15 questions to ascertain the needs of the librarian. At this point, there should be no demos, just questions and answers. In sales talk, this is an example of the consultative sales method. It is only after using this approach that the rep can even begin to think about offering a solution. Here are the types of questions that a librarian may be asked by the rep to determine need:

- Tell me about the work you do here.

- Are you satisfied with the service and data you are currently receiving from our company? How can we manage the relationship more effectively to ensure your satisfaction?

- Is your library serving your constituents 24/7? How is that working in relation to staffing? Are you effectively completing all the requested research?

- What is giving you the most "pain" in your daily activities as you serve the information needs of your internal clients here at the library?

- What are your long-term goals in the dissemination of information for your organization?

- Do you have responsibility for research globally or just in North America?

- Who are the key buyers of information in your organization? If we can demonstrate today that our information products have real relevance for you, how would these types of products be purchased?

- Can you tell me a little bit about the budget process?

- Are there CRM or tech people who need to get involved in the eventual purchase of the data?

- I noticed on your website that your library has a commitment to XYZ. Are you aware that we have many information products that deal with that in addition to the one you asked to see today?

Once the questions have been answered, it's up to the rep to review the answers with the information professional for clarity and accuracy as the next step unfolds. There are many more questions that could be asked, but 10 to 15 pertinent questions will give the salesperson a good idea of the needs of the library.

The sales rep is also an educator who helps the librarian to understand the nuances of the product. The rep may know of special deals and promotions that can be of great service to the information professional, in terms of both the usefulness of the data being presented and budgetary considerations. The buyer needs to understand how the product will meet the needs of the organization.

The librarian should have questions prepared as well. Conceptually, information professionals have to understand both their role and the role of the salesperson. Simply stated, one person sells and the other one buys.

Here are some questions that the librarian may ask of the sales rep:

- How does the coverage in this product compare to your competitors' products?

- Given that this is a new offering from your company, can you tell me about the research that went into its development?

- What is your commitment to service? We service branch libraries throughout the world. Are your customer service people available 24/7?

- If the technology associated with this product fails to operate effectively, what recourse is available to me from your company?

- What type of training do you provide?

- If I am interested in the product, can you give me more than just a 30-day trial?

- I'd like to have an open house at the library and feature your product for everyone to test it out. Will you be here for that day?

- If I am completely dissatisfied after a month or two, can I have my money back?

Review and Demonstrations

The next step in the sales meeting process is time for clarification, which should take 10 minutes. What was said? What was promised? What's next? All of these questions need to be answered.

Reading from her notes, the sales rep may say:

> "John, you indicated that your library runs 24 hours a day Monday through Friday, and from 8 AM to 8 PM on the weekends, servicing the U.S. and Canada. Is that correct?"
>
> "That's correct, Alice. We are well covered in North America, but our European library based in Paris is closed on the weekends, and, with the time difference, we cannot solve the information needs of our European offices from North America on a timely basis," the librarian would reply.
>
> Alice might reply, "Our company is open 24/7 and, as such, can cover the worldwide needs of your organization."

The rep will summarize the answers from the early part of the meeting and make sure that the information professional is in agreement as to the outstanding issues.

This could also be the time in the meeting for a demo of the product discussed. However, not all reps are proficient on all products, and therefore a demo should usually be left to the company's appropriate staff. Furthermore, it's best just to stay with the basics at this point, since no substantive plans for purchase have been discussed.

Under most circumstances, this is not the time to discuss price unless the rep knows how much funding is available, who the decision-makers are, and when a final decision will be made. Even if the information professional asks, "Can you give me a ballpark estimate of the cost to buy the databases you just presented?" the rep should not answer, because even though every database product offered by a company has a list price, if the salesperson is not given context as to what the library has in its budget to spend, then any number thrown out there is meaningless. Here's an example of how such a conversation might go:

> "Joe, can you give me a ballpark figure on what that database could cost me?"
> "Around $10,000," the rep might say.
> "Yikes, I don't have that much to spend!" the librarian says, walking away and never revealing the actual amount allocated for the purchase.

Again, waiting until all the details are known by both parties is the best time to negotiate price. See Chapter 5 for more on negotiating price.

Wrap-Up

At last, the sales rep has established a need, found out the approximate budget available for the purchase, ascertained the decision-making process, and suggested a product that would fill the needs of the library. At this point, the two parties will spend about 5 minutes wrapping things up, agreeing on their individual to-do lists and probably scheduling the next meeting or, at the very least, the next phone conversation.

KNOWLEDGE POINTS

- Both parties need to prepare a series of questions prior to the meeting.

- The information professional should ask just as many questions as the salesperson.

- If the rep tries to push a product before asking at least 10 questions, the information professional should tell him to wait until he knows what the library wants.

- Every sales meeting has four parts: introductions, fact-finding, review and demonstrations, and wrap-up.

- The info pro cannot let a talkative sales rep stray too far from the agenda.

- When the info pro asks for a "ballpark price" the rep should resist unless all the other factors, such as budget, close date, and so on, are known.

The Importance of Value

 "There's somethin' happenin' here, What it is ain't exactly clear," sang Buffalo Springfield in "For What It's Worth," written by Stephen Stills. While the lyrics bear no relation whatsoever to sales, the title does have relevance to the sales process. Because the question that ultimately needs to be answered is "What is your product worth to me?"

It's About Value, *Not* Price

Often, sales reps are unsuccessful in selling a product because they did not adequately explain what value the product could possibly have for the customer. Price always comes into the picture, but if the rep can demonstrate the value obtained by buying this product, price becomes a secondary discussion.

Let's start with a definition of value, according to *Webster's Collegiate Dictionary*:

1. Monetary worth: An amount expressed in money or another medium of exchange that is thought to be a fair exchange for something

2. Full recovered worth: The adequate or satisfactory return on or recompense for something

3. Worth of something: The worth, importance, or usefulness of something to somebody

One of the most common reasons sales reps give management when they don't get a sale is that the prospect had no money to spend. Really? The rep called the prospect, or the prospect called the rep, and they arranged a visit ostensibly for the rep to make a presentation and/or explain the features and benefits of a particular product. If the product didn't measure up to the competition's offerings, of course any sales manager would understand why that sale was lost. However, if the prospect is comparing like products (apples to apples, as they say), and the prices are comparable, the sales rep should not fail based on price. More likely, the rep's failure was based on an inability to demonstrate the value the product has for the library. Did the sales rep demonstrate the value before price was discussed? And on the other hand, did the information professional articulate to management the value expected from the product described by the rep?

Maybe it wasn't the price that caused the sale to fall through. Maybe the rep took the initial "no money" response as the final response and didn't probe as to what price the client would ultimately accept. The first "no" should not be the last "no."

The fact of the matter is, when customers tell a rep that the price is too high, what they are really saying is, "Give me a reason to buy," or in other words, "Show me the value." People will pay up to 15 percent more to buy a product or service if they want it, need it, *and* perceive great value in what is being sold. With competition lurking at every turn, sales reps need to give prospects not only a reason to buy but also a reason to work with the sales rep assigned to their account.

Let's go back to the excuse of losing the order due to price. Information professionals look at some very basic attributes of a product when making a buying decision, the most important aspect being product quality and the value it brings to the library. Once the question of quality is settled, then the next step is to clearly articulate "What is the perceived value of this product for the organization?" This is a key responsibility of the information professional. Of course, the rep should be probing to find this out, but if a rep fails to do so, then it is the info pro's responsibility to ask the relevant questions.

The reality is that, in our ultra-competitive world, there are always a few companies vying for the same customer base with similar products. It is therefore hard to believe that one company would price their offerings significantly higher—or lower—than their competition. It's just not smart to price yourself out of contention. After all, the marketplace really sets the price. With a sophisticated network of competitive intelligence, most companies know what their competitors' prices are. Therefore, no sale should be lost based on price.

Some salespeople complain that they lost a sale because the client for some unknown reason "hates us" and "loves our competitor." I had one rep caution me not to even try to do business with a certain consortium because the client was on the competitor's payroll. That was his explanation for continually coming up short on selling to this consortium.

"He's in their back pocket. He'll never do business with us even though we have better products than the competition," I was told. As it turned out, that client who preferred to work with the competition explained to me that the company I was working for had virtually forced him to go to the competition. For example, over the years, he often asked for price quotes that needed to be submitted to him within a specified time. The competition complied with that request while my company took weeks to complete the same task, and sometimes didn't even submit a quote—without explanation. Even with that dismal performance, the customer still continued to engage in conversation with us, hoping we would finally get our act together. Instead of complaining about a lack of love, the rep and the company need to figure out how to earn that love.

No senior sales executive should just accept the love–hate explanation of why a sale wasn't made. The situation needs to be investigated further. Of course, there may be isolated incidents where a company committed a major *faux pas* that caused the potential customer to prefer someone else. But be sensible: That love–hate explanation didn't even work in grade school when you told your mother that you got a C on a test because the teacher hated you, when really you just didn't study for the test and deserved the grade you got.

Similarly, customers don't hate your company; they just like your competitors better. I suggest that in the majority of cases where a contract is lost to a competitor, the losing side just didn't prepare properly. If sales reps figure out how to serve the customer better than the competition does, I guarantee that "hate" will miraculously turn into "love."

The successful sales rep understands the reality that price is not the ultimate consideration when a customer is deciding what to buy and from whom. Similar products from competing companies are usually priced within a ballpark range of one another. There are factors other than price that will ultimately determine the outcome.

On a recent consulting engagement, I called on an account in a mid-Atlantic state that was a significant customer of a company for which I had previously worked. At one point in the conversation, we spoke about a mutual friend of ours who is the head of a business library at a major Midwestern university. This customer told me that she sees our mutual friend at a meeting every year, in a city in the northeast. That was odd, considering the geographic locations of these two people. I learned that their annual get-together is sponsored by a company that brings in business school directors from all over the country for focus groups followed by a dinner for all the attendees. I said, "I'm sure your group has a few meetings like that with the other companies competing in the same vertical market."

She answered, "Not really."

That response told me that when an info pro is considering similar products from competing companies, the company that creates a strong relationship with the customer will usually win.

There are no tie scores in business. The company that has quality products, superior service, and knowledgeable salespeople who can create a strong bond with the customer will always win over its competitors.

Wise info pros should seek out companies that cater to their particular needs. Purchasing a product is not a one-time affair in the library world. Given that renewals are a basic part of the business, the library will see many people associated with the vendor as long as they keep renewing the product. It makes more sense to deal with a company that not only provides products with value but also listens to the info pro's opinions and makes changes to their product offerings based on that feedback. By creating this kind of bond, the info pro will get the highest quality products with the most value for the library patrons.

Features and Benefits

In order for a salesperson to convey the value of a product adequately and completely, he must clearly explain its features and benefits to the customer. One of the first concepts a newly hired salesperson learns is the difference between *features* and *benefits*.

A feature describes what a product has. Extra-wide tires on a sports car, for example, is a feature. The benefit is what that feature does for you. In the case of extra-wide tires, the car will hug the road more efficiently, and the car will be more responsive and drive more safely on winding roads.

None of us buys any product or service—at a store, in person, or online—based solely on features. We all buy based on our personal perception of what benefits we derive by making the purchase. The bottom line is that customers appreciate features, but they buy based on benefits.

When selling databases to libraries, the features describe what the product comprises: "Our new database on the environment covers 250 journals, hundreds of peer-reviewed articles, and examples of EPA cases that were successfully litigated." The benefit is that the patrons who use the library will have the most complete database of environmental information in the world.

For the information professional, understanding the concept of features vs. benefits will be most valuable during the sales meeting, particularly when discussing the product's merits with the salesperson:

> "Yes, Tom, I see the benefit to buying this because now the people who use the research library and need data to study oil-drilling in the Caspian Sea will have a database that is updated daily. That department has always had difficulty in finding up-to-date information. With this resource they will be far more efficient in publishing their findings."

To use value-added selling as a technique and a mode of operation, the info pro and the sales rep should do the following:

> Begin by talking about the
> Features
> then the
> Benefits
> which leads to determining how the
> Features and Benefits will solve/ease the
> Pain
> all of which ends up with a
> Solution

In other words, what solutions do the described benefits provide to ease the information professional's pain?

I would bet that virtually every company with a sales force has, most likely at the annual sales meeting, conducted a session on features vs. benefits. Companies add this module to the sales meeting agenda to drive home the concept of value-added selling. Newly hired reps appreciate the exercise and veterans always enjoy the refresher. Salespeople should ask the reps to pick three of their most popular products, three of their newest products, and three products that are not selling well. On a piece of paper, they should list one feature of each product and a few corresponding benefits:

FEATURE   BENEFITS

                               _____

_____   _____

                               _____

Similarly, this is a great exercise for the librarian in preparing for the sales meeting. The info pro should write the name of each product on a page, and list its features and their perceived related benefits. The info pro should bring this list to the meeting, and at the end of the meeting, review it to see if the rep has addressed the features and benefits of the products being presented.

This is a great exercise for the reps and librarians to better understand the features and benefits of specific products offered by the vendor. By completing this task, the reps gain a greater understanding of the products they are selling and the info pros get a better understanding of what they are buying and why.

The information professional can also look at the library's current database offerings to analyze their features and benefits, review those findings with colleagues, and then consider possible new additions to the collection. By engaging in this exercise, the info pro gains a features vs. benefits understanding that will serve him well when the sales rep arrives.

The 80/20 Rule

So many factors go into completing a successful sales process. Besides preparation by both parties prior to the meeting, inclusion of an agenda before every important meeting, and the understanding of features vs. benefits by both participants, many subtle facts overlooked or not understood may in fact torpedo all the good work just described. Most people are aware of the 80/20 rule, first identified by economist Vilfredo Pareto in Italy in 1896. After observing behaviors of members of Italian society, Pareto observed that "most people had little influence, power, or money in the marketplace." That group, which comprised some 80 percent of the population, he called the "trivial many," while the group that held all the influence and power in Italian society, the remaining 20 percent, he called the "vital few."

The fact is that the 80/20 rule is all around us: 80 percent of the earth is water, while 20 percent is comprised of land. In 1941, a management consultant named Joseph Juran began to study this principle and associate it with employee performance. The 80/20 rule is commonly referred to as The Pareto Principle.

In the sales context, this suggests that 20 percent of the people on a sales staff will bring in 80 percent of the company's sales. Those people would be best referred to as the "top producers." Moreover, salespeople are led to believe that 80 percent of their business comes from 20 percent of the highest revenue generating customers. And, finally, 80 percent of what a company produces is done equally as well as its competitors. It's the extra 20 percent of effort and unique content that differentiates a company from others selling similar products in the information industry.

On the library side, most libraries carry 80 percent of the same material. Most academic libraries have a standard and specific set of reference materials. Legal libraries, especially at major law firms, all carry similar reference materials. Corporate libraries, especially in competing industries, mirror each others' collections. What differentiates similar libraries in their collections is that 20 percent of unique materials that may not be resident in the other libraries. Academic libraries, for example, are constantly trying to attract the best and the brightest students and faculty to their campus. So a major selling point for them would be to offer unique collections pertinent to a specific field of study that many competing institutions may not have.

That unique 20 percent may not seem to be a lot, but it can be the difference between closing a big deal or not, and between attracting a prominent faculty member or not.

KNOWLEDGE POINTS

- When the customer tells the sales rep, "Your price is too high," what he really means is, "Show me the value."

- It's the product, the rep, and then the company that provide the cumulative basis for a customer's decision on what to buy (or not). If all three are of the highest quality, a sale is probable.

- If a salesperson says he lost the sale due to price, management needs to investigate further. Price should never be the deterrent in finalizing a sale.

- Features vs. benefits is always worth reviewing.

- Information professionals should use the features vs. benefits exercise for two purposes: to better understand the worth of their current collections, and to gain a better understanding of any products they intend to purchase.

- Twenty percent makes the difference between just getting by and winning. For a little more effort, you will get so much more in return.

Breaking Down the Barriers

When you hear the expression, "The customer is always right," do you wonder if that is really true? It is. As a salesperson, if you don't understand that concept and wholeheartedly believe it, you need to be in another line of work.

The job of salespeople is to serve the customer. This often requires thinking outside the box about how to help clients. However, success at actually implementing positive change rests with management. At some companies where I worked, I was lucky to have incredible support from management. At other times, I was not as fortunate. Whether management is supportive or not, a sales rep should never stop trying to think creatively and should continue to bring new and fresh ideas to management for consideration, so that the customer can be better served.

The bottom line is that the customer is, in fact, always right. Customers are right even when they are wrong. The job of salespeople is to provide service with a smile. After all, if it weren't for customers, salespeople would not be employed; and if there are no jobs, they have no income; and if they have no income, well, you know the rest.

Information professionals also have customers: the people who use library services and those who hold the purse strings. Much of what salespeople know about pleasing their customers is applicable to the library's internal customers as well.

Perceived and Real Barriers

My first sales job involved selling microfiche copies of Securities and Exchange Commission (SEC) documents to libraries on a yearly subscription basis. Public companies are required by law to file these documents with the government. They have 90 days from the end of their fiscal year to get this information to the SEC. An integral part of our contract with the government was that each and every document subscribed to *had* to be delivered to the customer within 10 days of being filed at the SEC. If we failed to live up to that part of the agreement, we would be in breach of contract and conceivably could have the business taken away from us.

As a result of that contract requirement, the company put in place an elaborate system to make sure that the fiche was delivered on time, every time. Every librarian that I ever visited knew that their documents would be delivered within 10 days or less of their SEC filing. No ifs, ands, or buts!

The reality was that we rarely had complaints on timeliness of delivery. The company always did an excellent job in this area. However, the other reality was that, due to filing date requirements, certain documents filed at specific times of the year wreaked havoc with the system because of the sheer volume of paper being filed at the SEC. For example, the 10-K, which had the most complete information of any of the documents, was required to be filed within 90 days of the end of the company's fiscal year. Since the majority of companies had a December 31 year-end date, the bulk of anyone's 10-K subscription would arrive at the end of March or beginning of April.

Early one year, I closed an order for a one-person corporate library to receive every 10-K from every public company. The customer authorized the form in the morning, and, as I was comfortably sitting at my desk that afternoon basking in my self-glory and processing the order, she called me:

> "Mike, you said that approximately 75 to 80 percent of my 10-K's subscription will probably arrive throughout the month of April. Is that correct?" she asked.
>
> "Yes, given the nature of that particular document and the SEC's filing requirement, you can expect to see the bulk of your subscription arrive during the month of April," I said.
>
> She paused—a silence for what seemed forever—and then said, "I'm sorry, but I must cancel my order."
>
> The last thing any salesperson wants to hear is the dreaded three words, "Cancel my order." So naturally I asked "Why?"
>
> "I am a one-person library," she said, "which means that in addition to answering reference questions and conducting research, I also have to reshelve the books, and now I will have to file the fiche as well. If so many fiche arrive in a 30-day period, I will never be able to file them on time and effectively—which means they will be useless. My patrons will not be able to use them because the fiche will be sitting in boxes and not out for public use," she said with concern and dismay.
>
> "So the problem is filing? It's not with the information you'll be receiving?"
>
> "Yes, if I can't file them, no one can use them," she said, spoken as a true and conscientious information professional.

My order was quickly evaporating due to the librarian's lack of time for filing. The order was not being canceled due to price or inadequacy of the product. It had nothing to do with features or benefits. It was in jeopardy because this librarian did not have the staff to help her file the fiche.

The solution to the dilemma immediately seemed clear to me. I offered to provide her with a person at no cost to her library to file the fiche for a few hours every day throughout the month of April. I knew that local library schools had a number of MLS students who needed extra income. The incremental cost to me to get someone to file the fiche was negligible in light of the total dollar value of the new business that I saw slipping away. That order was not going down the drain if I could help it. If I couldn't get a student to do the filing, I would have done it myself to help the customer and save the order.

I contacted Pratt Institute, a well-known library school in the New York area. Pratt sent over a delightful young man to do the filing. He was a library student and did such a great job for the customer that we subsequently hired him to work for our company when he graduated from library school.

We saved the order, satisfied the client—who remained a client for many years—and helped a young library student, creating a gigantic win–win situation for everyone.

Sometimes words from an associate or supervisor help a situation where thinking out of the box was needed to save a renewal. A significant part of the work being done by a sales rep in the information industry is the task of renewing accounts. Both renewals and new business are the main components of a rep's compensation. Therefore, the thought of a customer not renewing is upsetting for most reps in our industry.

The head of the library that I sold to on the west coast was Vladimir, who originated from Eastern Europe. At that time, his library was spending a significant sum of money with my company, which meant that he was a valued customer and that I spent a considerable amount of time in contact with Vladimir. Frequent phone calls, emails, and at least two to three trips out to the coast was my "modus operandi "in servicing this account.

Around renewal time, Vladimir called me, and his tone was urgent. Our talk went something like this:

> "Hello Mike! You are really in the soup this time!" he said. The visual of me drowning in a big pot of vegetables, matzo balls, chicken bones, and broth was not very pleasant.
>
> "Oh, hello, Vladimir. How are you today?" I asked trying to recover from his first comment.
>
> "Mike, I am not kidding around! Your competitor has contacted my boss and the dean of business and told them that your price for the exact same information is four times more than his. I am getting nasty memos telling me to cancel your service in favor of this guy. You better come out here immediately!" he demanded.
>
> "I'll be out there next Wednesday" I said without a moment's hesitation since I knew my boss would make himself available for this client.

I called my boss and we agreed to meet on the west coast the following Wednesday. I would take the first flight out of New York, which would get me to the coast at approximately 11:30 in the morning. He would arrive on the west coast before me, rent a car, and pick me up at the airport.

The following Wednesday, I was with my boss in a rental car on our way to the appointment that I was not looking forward to:

> "So, Mike tell me about this guy," my boss inquired as we turned on to the interstate.
>
> "Out of all my customers, there is something about this guy. I think he's OK, but I never feel entirely comfortable when I meet with him. It's almost as though there is a big thorn in the chair I'm sitting in. I mean, we don't have disagreements—up until now—

but for the most part we have a cordial, not entirely a warm relationship," I said.

Thinking a bit further, I said "This guy is probably the only customer I have ever worked with that intimidates me."

We then spoke about our strategy for the meeting. We wrote down our objectives, mapped out the solutions we would present, and felt pretty satisfied that we could calm his fears, secure the renewal, and maybe walk out with a sale of a new product we were introducing the following month.

After I introduced my boss to Vladimir and went through the usual pre-meeting pleasantries, we probed as to what he was looking for from us. The meeting was unusually long and after more than 2 hours, the three of us were smiling. Vladimir got what he wanted, and we got the renewal and even sold him that new product.

As we were leaving, my boss turned to Vladimir and said, "You know on the way over here, Mike told me an interesting thing about you. He said that you are the only customer he has ever worked with that intimidates him."

Vladimir visibly blushed and said, "I can't believe it. I have always had productive meetings and conversations with Mike. I would never purposely do anything to make him feel uncomfortable."

Of course, I was speechless and pretty much cannot remember what I then told Vladimir. We quickly left with orders in hand and virtually no words could exit from my mouth until we drove a few miles in the rental car.

"Intimidated?" I blurted out.

"Hey, you said it, I just repeated it," my boss calmly replied. "Look, by doing what I just did, I removed the barriers to your relationship with Vladimir. From now on, he will treat you better, and you will work together even more efficiently than before."

My boss had a remarkable talent for sizing up a situation and then quickly figuring out how to deal with it. Those few words used judiciously eliminated the small barrier between Vladimir and me. As a result, we did have a much better business relationship and his library remained a major customer for many years thereafter.

Technical Barriers

When I was the director of academic sales for the first company I worked for, Disclosure, the prime sales target market was universities with MBA programs. In addition to calling on the libraries and business schools themselves, we worked closely with the AACSB, the business school accreditation organization. AACSB would publish a handbook of approved collegiate schools of business. Using that book, I contacted almost all of them, made the expected sales calls, and brought in the business.

I was once given a new product to sell that resided on a floppy disk (remember those?). This program took public company financial information from all the New York and American Stock Exchange companies and provided an incredibly detailed monetary analysis of their reported earnings. It was a very slick product, and I knew instinctively that it would be a great seller to my prime customers and prospects.

After I had made some initial presentations with this new tool in hand, it became all too clear that I had a major problem. Everyone I showed it to liked it and wanted to buy it. However, at that time, nobody had suitable computer equipment to run the program. Hard as it is to believe today, the use of computers in classes and libraries was in its infancy then. Computer equipment was very costly and, in many cases, simply unavailable, due to lack of inventory and limited university budgets.

At one of my weekly meetings with my boss, I recounted to him how everyone liked the product but couldn't make the purchase because they all lacked sufficient computer equipment to run it. Offhandedly I remarked that the only way I could sell this product was to give it away or package a computer with every sale.

His eyes lit up, and I saw the light bulb switch on over his blonde head when he said, "Great idea, Mike!"

"Hmm, there was an idea there?" I asked him to elaborate on my supposed idea.

He decided we should, in fact, package computer equipment along with the product. That discussion led to me to conduct a brief marketing study to determine how many AACSB accredited schools of business were real prospects, how many of those prospects were already customers, how many more would buy that were not customers already, and what the predicted total number of sales would be over a 3-year period. We decided that we would package the floppy disk product with the latest IBM computer equipment and even include a printer. The customer in return would agree to a 3-year commitment, one third paid each year. At the end of the 3-year term, ownership of all the equipment would be transferred to the customer.

Once we had studied the situation and created the sales analysis, we presented our plan to the owners of Disclosure. They liked the idea and gave us the approval to proceed. Disclosure became the largest seller of IBM computer equipment in the Washington, DC-area, because we were able to sell the product packaged with IBM equipment to a large number of university libraries that supported MBA programs. We not only made the sale, but our efforts brought high-end computers into libraries, thus serving the needs of both the library and business school. In some cases, university libraries prevailed upon us to include two or three computer systems with their purchase. I was fortunate to work for forward-thinking management in a company with supportive ownership.

KNOWLEDGE POINTS

- The job of the salesperson is to serve the customer.

- Both sales reps and information professionals need to be mindful that the customer is always right.

- Barriers exist in selling a product, buying a product, and making sure the technology works in a product. Additionally, barriers exist in the relationship between sales rep and info pro. Both sides need to recognize those barriers exist and work to eliminate them.

- Both sales reps and information professionals need to be creative and think outside the box, for their mutual benefit.

THREE

CLOSING THE SALE

"Money," written and performed by the British band Pink Floyd, is the song that for me best exemplifies closing the sale: the sound of the cash register and the coins dropping in the song, along with the lyrics, "Money, it's a gas, Grab that cash with both hands and make a stash."

This section examines the final steps of the buying and selling process: decision-making and closing the sale. A new series of touch points comes into play for both the rep and librarian. How long will this process take, from the time when the final quote is given to the time when the library or consortium announces the winning bid? In other words, what is everyone's expectation with regard to the timeline of the decision-making process, and how can that process be effectively managed?

During this stage, negotiation begins. For information professionals, negotiating with a vendor can be a tricky situation. In this section, I will present ideas to level the playing field, so that both parties can derive an equitable outcome.

And, finally, this section covers what happens post-sale, because once the sale has been completed, the real work begins. After all, most database products are sold to libraries on a subscription basis. That means that at the very least the library can inevitably expect the salesperson who originally sold the product or a new salesperson to contact the library 90 to 120 days before the subscription lapses to obtain the renewal. But beyond that, after the sale, who does what to ensure satisfaction?

11

Managing the
Decision-Making Process

> ♪ Sometimes you don't need lyrics in a song to convey an idea.
> I am reminded of the popular hit television series *Jeopardy*,
> hosted by Alex Trebek. The theme, written by the show's
> creator the late Merv Griffin, is a universal melody that connotes
> someone deep in thought about to make a decision. I can hear
> it now ... and the correct question to the answer is ...

Once the presentations have been made and the proposed prices finalized, the last and perhaps most important phase of the buying-and-selling process takes over: decision-making. It is not as obvious as in presenting and pricing, but during that period of time when a final decision is to be made, *diplomacy* and *tact* are the watchwords. Careless words, improper communication, and lack of attention to detail can subvert even an order that everyone thought was "in the bag."

Throughout all the stages of the buying and selling process, but especially in the final decision-making phase, clear expectations need to be set for both parties. On the sales side, the rep needs to make sure that all the divisions of the company that have contact with the customer are efficiently managed. For example, a festering customer service issue may have a negative effect on a pending order if the customer feels that issue has not been handled properly. A customer has every right to delay buying, or not to buy, a new product if technical or customer service issues are not being dealt with to his satisfaction.

The info pro, on her side of the process, needs to make sure the library's expectations and requirements are spelled out to the vendor. The library is holding all the cards at this point because the vendor knows that a sale is on the horizon and is usually willing to be as generous as possible to make the deal happen. It's up to the library to use this crucial time to extract whatever accommodations from the vendor it can in order to get the best possible deal.

Clarifying Expectations

A critical part of the decision-making process is making sure expectations are clear on both sides. Let's consider the following example: Jane is a sales rep selling a baseball database to a library, at which Lynn is her contact. Jane has made the presentations and involved her management to obtain the best possible price for her customer, and the decision is now in the hands of the library committee.

At this point, the info pro needs to clearly inform the sales rep of the library's decision-making process and the expected time frame, as shown in this statement from Lynn:

> "Jane, thank you for the price quotes for your new baseball database. We appreciate the time spent and the presentations made. When purchased, this will be a valuable addition to our sports management section of the library. We will have a decision on whether the acquisitions committee approves this sale in approximately 2 months. I will call you as soon as possible with our decision, but it looks like we have at least 60 days or more before a final decision is made."

At this point, for the sales rep, it's all about respecting Lynn's ground rules. Lynn's statement seems to tell Jane that she should back off until a decision is made in approximately 2 months.

It's up to Jane to keep her management informed as to when they might possibly expect an order. Sometimes salespeople are uncomfortable telling management that an order that was expected momentarily will not happen for a few months. But if the info pro has shared a time frame for when the order may be finalized, then it is the rep's responsibility to accurately convey that fact to management.

Being cognizant of the rules of engagement between the rep and librarian can be critical to the completion of a sale. If the contact at the library says that there is no need to call because the decision-making is out of her hands, then the rep for the most part should abide by those instructions.

Of course, if a rep does decide to check up, it's all in the presentation. For example, Jane may call Lynn and say, "Hi, I'm just checking in with you. Anything new to report?" This is a friendly and nonconfrontational way for the sales rep to inquire about the status of the intended order without saying anything overtly about it or asking where the order is in the pipeline. The information professional is fully aware that the rep is somewhat anxious about the status of the order and usually will do everything possible to be supportive without revealing any inside information. So perhaps Lynn simply replies, "No word yet, but I am looking forward to adding that resource to our collection." In this case, the rep and the librarian have made contact, even if the result is nothing more than a pleasant exchange.

On the other hand, I have seen reps unwittingly torpedo their orders by resorting to heavy-handed tactics in this kind of situation. What if Jane took this approach?

> "Lynn, if that order isn't in my hands by Friday, I cannot extend the discount I offered," demands Jane.
>
> "Really, Jane? I guess I'll take my chances if that deadline you just gave me passes. Can't make promises for something I don't know about," Lynn may say.

The bottom line is that the information professional knows that, when the order eventually comes in, the rep will most certainly extend the discount. By resorting to coercive tactics, the rep has driven a wedge into the relationship she is trying to cultivate with the librarian.

Again, it all comes down to managing the expectations to prepare for the outcome. Since the order will be coming from the library, it's up to the librarian to manage the process. Once the final price has been submitted along with the accompanying contractual agreements, the librarian is fully in control. Yes, Exalted Information Professional, it's now *your* show.

The info pro can and should set the ground rules for contact during the decision-making period. By doing so, she is managing expectations and outcomes. In fact, in an RFP approval system, most institutions will not respond to sales rep inquiries during the decision-making process.

Going back to the example with Jane and Lynn, Lynn's initial statement implies that Jane should not call this prospect before a decision is handed down by the committee. If Jane does call, she will likely not get an answer and her actions may only serve to annoy Lynn. On the other hand, if Jane has followed up with Lynn and asked for permission to make status calls along the way, then it is fine for her to call her contact.

Regardless of the amount of communication agreed to, reps should always be available during the process for any last-minute details that need clarification. Similarly, librarians also need to be available for any questions that somehow eluded answers earlier.

Understanding Sales Requirements and Payment Plans

It is necessary for the rep to ascertain what requirements the target library has when it is buying information and for the info pro to share this information with the rep. Libraries have a limitless variety of methods for ordering products and services. The rep needs to understand precisely how the library plans to do business with the company. Moreover, it's the rep's responsibility to make sure the intended customer understands the vendor's procedure when accepting an order.

A good way for the information professional to help move the process along is to accurately inform the rep of the way in which an order (new and renewal) gets processed at that organization. By knowing the procedures and quirks of the purchasing institution ahead of time, the rep can manage the sale more effectively, and the time spent on processing the sale will be greatly reduced.

Furthermore, some libraries require certain information before they consider conducting business with a vendor. For example, they may require that a vendor have minority or female ownership or, if that is not the case, include minority- or female-owned businesses as part of the vendor's team.

Similarly, some vendors have extensive paperwork that a customer must complete. The vendor may refuse to accept an order if the paperwork is not properly filled out by the customer. Of course, having a sale held "on acceptance" of paperwork is a sales rep's worst nightmare, so making sure both parties understand the paperwork portion of the order process is quite important.

The rep needs to alert the library as to what paperwork the vendor requires in order to do business. While one would imagine that a vendor would do everything possible to simplify the ordering process, some companies nevertheless require a multitude of documents with an inordinate number of pages to be authorized by the customer.

For the info pro, understanding what types of payment plans the company accepts is critical, and the rep should make these options clear. Some companies are more lenient than others in granting extended terms of payment. For example, companies who sell their products and services to nonprofit state institutions are fully aware that payment can take from 90 to 120 days. They know that the state library or the state university is good for the money and understand that internal paperwork requirements have a tendency to extend receipt of payment.

The ground rules on how business is to be conducted for both the salesperson and the information professional need to be clearly spelled out, so that when the sale is finally made, the order can be processed and the library can begin to receive the data.

Once the Decision Is Made

The big day finally arrives, and the librarian calls the rep to say that the committee has made a "buy" decision. If, in its infinite wisdom, the committee has chosen the product from that salesperson's company, then it's great news!

But, as we all know, there can only be one winner. The vendor that is not chosen is of course expected to be gracious in defeat. However, when this news is conveyed, the rep who did not win the contract should inquire as to why the library decided to purchase someone else's product. Only through healthy communication with the librarian can the salesperson understand how the company fell short and how the sales rep might improve the offering next time. In sales, you win some and lose some. The wise salesperson takes note of a setback and tries to determine how to do better next time. In sports, business, and politics, people who were once at the top of their profession fall from grace. Many learn from whatever it was that threw them how to get back on track. If a rep loses a sale, she should learn from the experience so as to do better next time. Many managers conduct a "post-mortem" meeting after a major sale is lost, not to chastise the rep, but to analyze what went wrong so it can be corrected in the future.

In addition to closing the loop with the successful rep, the info pro needs to coach the rep whose company did not get the order on how to do better the next time. It's through this process of mutual understanding that salespeople and information professionals learn to work more closely together. Today's loss may be tomorrow's win.

KNOWLEDGE POINTS

- During decision-making, the information professional is in total control of the negotiation process.

- Heavy-handed tactics by the sales rep will most certainly not help to get the order any sooner and, in fact, could jeopardize it.

- In finalizing an order both the rep and the librarian need to be in agreement on how each is managing the decision-making process for their respective sides.

- By sharing the procedural requirements prior to final approval, both the rep and the information professional will pave the way for smooth and efficient processing of the order.

- The info pro can act as a coach to help the sales rep of the losing company do better the next time his product is up for consideration.

12

Negotiating Skills

♪ "It's Your Thing" was a song released in 1969, written and sung by one of my favorite R&B groups, the Isley Brothers. It proclaims freedom: "It's your thing, Do what you wanna do. I can't tell you, who to sock it to." The Brothers were not referring to librarians in the song, but for the purpose of making a point in this chapter, librarians, negotiation is *your* thing.

Elements of Negotiation for the Information Professional

Salespeople are well trained in the art of negotiating. Their employers are fully aware of the competition from other vendors and will present the sales staff with compelling arguments to use as to why their solution is the best to fulfill the library's needs. Vendors devote a considerable amount of money each year to teaching their salespeople and key executives the fine art of negotiating with librarians.

For librarians, on the other hand, negotiation can be the most difficult part of the buying and selling process. At every session I conduct on negotiations skills for information professionals, the first question I ask is "How much money is earmarked by your library to train you on negotiation skills?" Inevitably the answer is none.

Nevertheless, librarians are expected to negotiate with many different types of information providers for a variety of products and services. Whether the library is purchasing content, furniture, consulting, or technology, the info pro can expect a whole host of vendors to beat a path to his door. If he is not fully prepared, or at least conversant in the basics of negotiation skills and practices, the process will be less than fulfilling for both parties.

At face value, most vendors will present products and services that are completely adequate for purchase by the library. The key for the information professional is to be able to sift through the extraneous information so as to find the right product for the right price.

Libraries represent an incredibly lucrative market for information database vendors. In Outsell's *2010 Information Industry Market Size, Share & Forecast Report* (www.outsellinc. com/store/products/968-2010-information-industry-market-size-share-forecast-report), it was estimated that information providers to libraries represented a $368.5 billion market. Moreover, the report predicted that this number would be rising, not declining.

Furthermore, for virtually every information database available, there are three or four similar databases offered by other companies at similar prices. What this means is that when contemplating the purchase of a database or any other service, an info pro does not have to accept the first offer given by a vendor and, in most cases, can turn to another vendor that offers a similar product.

The information industry is growing. Libraries provide billions of dollars to a finite group of vendors that sell information products. The vendors are fully cognizant of the importance of the library market to their revenue streams. They invest large sums of money in training their salespeople and senior executives on the finer points of negotiation because they know that their librarian customers have incredible leverage when the negotiations begin and they want their sales reps to be fully prepared so that the business does not get shifted to another vendor.

The librarian's leverage can be used to negotiate favorable terms in the following areas.

Price: Is it a renewal or new sale? In the information industry, most databases are sold on a subscription basis. Much like selling insurance, selling data is an annuity business, which means that the service is renewed each year along with a modest price increase, thus generating sales for the company and commissions for the salesperson. (While many librarians may think that renewing a service should cost the same as or less than the initial price, vendor costs go up every year in efforts to improve the product, develop better technology, and pay for employees that provide product support. Just as with most goods purchased by consumers, increased costs get passed onto the customer.)

If it's a new product being sold, commonly referred to in sales parlance as "new business," depending on the company's sales goals, there is a good chance that a lower-than-advertised price can be negotiated. And, by the way, any time price is discussed, the information professional has every right to ask how that price was determined. "By the way, do you have a price sheet that you can leave with me here at the library?" is a question that should be asked by the library contact. The rep should be able to provide a valid reason for the proposed price (i.e., the price should be defensible).

However, be it a new sale or renewal, price is always the *last* topic discussed in a negotiation. After the info pro has voiced her needs, and the salesperson has understood those needs and confirmed that they are addressed by the product, then and only then can the topic of price be approached. Many a sale has been lost because the price was discussed before there was a firm understanding of everyone's needs and objectives. "Sam, can you give me a ballpark figure of how much that database will cost? I won't hold you to it," the librarian may say. If the rep does not yet know the full details of the library's needs and budget, giving a price here may very well kill the deal.

Payment options: Vendors are only too happy to acquire the library's business, and sometimes the only way to get that business is to offer payment options. Two- and three-year commitments often qualify for vendor discounts. Semi-annual payments can be established with some of the more enlightened vendors.

Many times academic institutions get "year-end" monies that need to be spent in a relatively short period of time. The vendor who can get an invoice out to the customer in a short period of time is the one who will get this type of business. I used to get calls every December from certain clients who had "year-end" money to spend, but to get the sale I had to get an invoice on the librarian's desk in 48 hours. Good reps never miss a deadline like that!

Performance guarantees: We are all entitled to buy cars that last over 10K miles, clothing that won't wear out after one washing, and shoes whose soles don't need to be replaced every month. And when buying databases, an info pro has the right and responsibility to insist that performance guarantees be written into the signed agreement. Technology is moving just as fast for the vendor as it is for the library, so a database, platform, or technology developed with all good intentions may have some bugs in the system. It happens! The vendor needs to stand behind the product or technology, and the info pro needs to ask for that guarantee.

Additional months of coverage for no extra fee: A great way for a library to achieve more of a discount is for the librarian to ask for a free trial prior to buying the product. If the info pro wants to buy a certain database, she can ask for a 30-, 60-, or 90-day trial to precede the 12-month subscription. If the salesperson knows that the sale is a foregone conclusion, extended free trials are usually granted without much of a fuss.

Remote access/world access: With the ever-increasing changes in today's employment market, many companies and institutions offer employees a work-at-home option. Remote access is a fact of life today, and info pros who need this option should request that option from their salesperson. If a company is unwilling to allow for remote access at no additional cost, then you may want to do business elsewhere.

Cap on renewal percentage increase: Another way for the info pro to control costs is to ask for a clause in the agreement that caps renewal increases over the "out" years, so they do not exceed a certain percentage. For example, "Harry, we want to order this database and expect to have it here for at least 3 years; therefore, I don't want my renewal percentage to increase by more than 2 percent per year." If the vendor truly wants your business, this type of request is usually granted.

The vendor will attempt to minimize these kinds of requests as much as possible, but in the realm of buying and selling and negotiating, there must be some give and take from both sides. Therefore, throughout the entire process, the information professional should have a game plan with the following four elements (Figure 12.1):

1. Setting objectives

2. Setting a timetable

3. Assembling a team

4. Developing a strategy

Setting Objectives

The info pro needs to set goals and objectives regarding the contract, for example:

- While only a 12-month commitment is needed, the best deal will include 2 to 3 months extra at no additional cost, in other words, 15 months for the price of 12.

- Renewal should be capped at no more than a 3 percent price increase every year.

- Performance guarantees must be included.

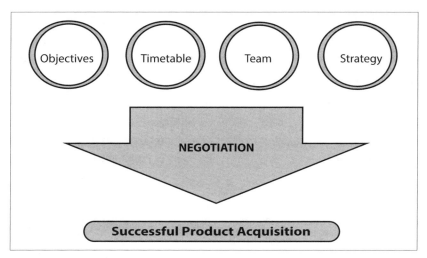

Figure 12.1   The steps to successful product acquisition (©2012 Matt Dunie and Mike Gruenberg)

The list goes on and on, but these are representative examples of some conditions that a librarian may want to include in the final agreement. Most important is to write those objectives down early in the process and update the list as negotiations proceed.

Setting a Timetable

It cannot be stressed enough that the time spent on negotiations and the time allotted for a final decision rests squarely in the hands of the librarian. Naturally, the vendor has a timetable as well, but it is dependent on the info pro's. To complete an effective negotiation, the information professional must adhere to a schedule that has been carefully established with the library's goals in mind.

Figure 12.2 is a chart that shows all the steps in a negotiation, from initial inquiry to the final approval of the order. In essence, this is a "living document" that will be updated as the process of negotiating unfolds over time.

Research, Team, Trial, Align Budget, Conditions, Success Metrics, Approval

Time	1	2	3	4
Inquiry				
	Research	Research		
	Team	Document Objectives	Establish Success Measures	
		Determine Value	Align Budget	
			Feasibility	
			Conditions	
		Evaluate		Price
				Contract Items
				Approval

Figure 12.2 Steps to negotiation (© 2012 Matt Dunie and Mike Gruenberg)

However, the key element for info pros to remember is that the timetable belongs to them. For example, the rep may say that he needs the order signed and in house by the end of the year. However, if the company's year end is December 31 but the library's is July 31, the library's end of the year is the one that matters.

Assembling a Team

Information professionals are not alone in the negotiation process; or rather they are only alone if they choose to be. It is far better to assemble a team than to go one-on-one with the vendor. Within the library there are content experts and technology experts, and some of them may have dealt previously with the prospective vendor. Assemble a team, utilize their thoughts, and elicit their advice. The team will help to shape the questions and review the answers, so that instead of rushing into a decision, the library can acquire an appropriate product in a specified amount of time.

Figure 12.3 shows an example of a chart of possible team members assembled for a library–vendor negotiation, with every possible aspect of the negotiation covered by an expert from the library.

Position	Responsibility	Name
Team leader	Organizes everything	YOU
Financial authority	All finance, budget, payment	Money Bags
Technology	Technical due diligence	Geek Squad
Expertise	Discipline specific	Mr. Know-It-All
Legal	Legal	Legal Beagle
Supervisor	Oversight	The Boss

Figure 12.3 Potential team members for negotiation (© 2012 Matt Dunie and Mike Gruenberg)

Developing a Strategy

The final piece of the puzzle is to develop and implement a strategy, which means going back to the objectives. The objectives should serve as a checklist and reminder throughout the process, and will consistently change as the information professional works through the negotiation process. The objectives as initially written sometime bear little resemblance to the final outcome.

Important Reminder for the Sales Reps

As I wrote this chapter, I had a vision of some sales reps saying sarcastically, "Hey, thanks Mike, for giving these tips to librarians for negotiating with us." But the bottom line is that if both sides are more aware, and mindful of one another, the negotiation process will ultimately work more effectively for everyone.

Salespeople want library people to succeed and vice versa. By understanding each other's roles, we eliminate the nonsense and get down to the issues at hand.

Handling Objections in Negotiations

While I've never actually seen an information professional or sales rep screaming "No can do!" during a negotiation, I have been in negotiations where the objections far outweighed the common ground. Clearly voicing the issues at hand can help participants get past the emotionalism and showmanship, and usually calms everyone down.

The road to agreement can be a rocky one. I have noticed that with one-on-one negotiations, consisting of just the rep and the customer, the results usually are arrived at relatively quickly, with a fair outcome. When there is a crowd of people on both sides of the table, some of the participants may feel the need to assert themselves, to let everyone know who is the top dog in the room. That's when trouble can rear its ugly head.

Many years ago, I managed a salesperson named Albert who covered the accounting and legal markets for our company. A major accounting firm requested that both he and I appear at their office to discuss their impending renewal. Apparently, the customer was somewhat upset that the price of the renewal had gone up by 2.5 percent over the previous year. Albert was nervous about the meeting because his contact in the library there had told him that internal memos were circulating throughout the firm making it clear that expenses needed to be cut. This was a high-dollar renewal, and we were prime candidates to take a revenue cut. We were easy targets.

Albert and I reviewed the company's usage and determined that our data was being used extensively throughout the firm. We also reviewed the past 5 years of renewal payments and calculated that, over that period, our price increase amounted to less than 1 percent per year. Clearly, we had a very compelling story to tell, and I felt confident that we would secure the renewal with a price increase somewhere between 1.5 and 2.5 percent.

On the day of the meeting, we were ushered into a large conference room on the 45th floor of a Park Avenue building. If the company was trying to demonstrate frugality and cost-cutting, this room was not the one in which to plead the case—wood-paneled, well-appointed, with at least 20 chairs, the latest audiovisual conferencing system, and a table set with soda, ice, water, and coffee.

There were five people in the room when we entered. Three were men I had never met before and the fourth was our contact from the library, whom I had known for a number of years. The fifth was a woman who never spoke nor was she introduced to us. She just took notes.

As we sat across from one another and made the obligatory introductions, I sensed that this was not going to be a pleasant conversation. After the initial introductions, the person who appeared to be in charge began to speak:

> "My name is Bob 'Bud' Smith, and I've been hired by
> the partners to look into cost-cutting here at the firm,"
> he said with great conviction.

There was a collective nod of agreement by all of the people sitting with Bud.

Not wanting to get the conversation started on the wrong foot, I acknowledged that in tough economic times, realistic cost-cutting is an option that should be employed at all firms and not just the Fortune 500 ones.

> "That's right, and that's why we asked that you and
> Albert come to visit us today. Quite frankly, I am
> outraged by your prices," he said defiantly.
>   "With all due respect, our prices have remained at
> less than a 1 percent increase per year, and the usage

of our data at the firm has risen by 23 percent over that same 5-year period" I said.

"You may be right, but that doesn't address how much we are spending today. The partners want to cut costs, and my job is to send a crystal clear message to all their vendors."

Albert was sitting next to me. I noticed little beads of sweat appearing on his forehead as he started to see this six-figure renewal float out the 45th-floor window. I had assured him before the meeting that this renewal was not going to go away. They needed our data, they were heavily using our data, and the librarian was very supportive of us.

To placate Bud and bring this thing to a conclusion, I took the following approach:

"Look, why we don't just finalize the renewal at a 1 percent increase so as to account for a modest cost-of-living increase and call it a day."

Bud replied, "Why don't you cut your price in half, and we'll call it a day?" Not the response I was looking for.

"Your firm is receiving excellent service from us. I have with me the customer service reports that show your employees around the world consistently complimenting us on the service they are receiving. Our prices are reasonable, and the renewal increase is almost nothing. As VP of sales, I have a certain degree of flexibility in negotiating price. Cutting the price by 50 percent is not within the guidelines that I can approve," I said.

"If you can't approve it, will you take that offer to senior management at your company?" he asked.

"In all good conscience, I cannot and will not insult the senior management and ownership of my company with that offer. Therefore the answer is no, I won't convey this offer, and no, I cannot accept it on any level. Thank you for your time."

I paused, motioned to Albert to pack up his papers as I did the same, and we both got up from our chairs. As we opened the door to leave, Bud asked us to stay. We spoke a little longer, and I told him again how much we could discount the renewal. I confirmed that I would follow up my offer in writing and that the offer was good for 30 days.

Less than a week later, Albert picked up the renewal, which was at a 1 percent price increase over the previous year. Our company got less than it wanted and Bud got less than he wanted, but we both came away with a win.

Most negotiations are not this melodramatic or confrontational. I felt that I had to handle Bud's objections in a manner that exhibited strength and resolve. In subsequent discussions I had with him, he turned out to be a pretty decent guy.

The first step in handling objections on either side of the table is to recognize them. Bud said our product was too expensive. My response at that point was to express understanding of what he said. At no point did I argue with him. I then proceeded to offer alternatives to get his agreement and move toward finalizing the deal.

Handling objectives is a four step process:

1. Let the other person know that you understand his concern.

2. Show appreciation of the other person's views.

3. Give alternatives, whether it's about price, billing considerations, or something else.

4. Move to agreement and understand this is a give-and-take process.

When Negotiations Don't Work

Negotiations are complicated, and every negotiation involves multiple sets of ideas that will continually change until all issues are resolved. When the customer raises an objection, the salesperson needs to acknowledge it and work toward settling the issue. Being argumentative will not help, and for a negotiation to work best, both parties need to have their facts documented and well prepared in advance of the meeting.

Alas, however, some negotiations stall or never really get off the ground. The librarian needs to know when to quit. Sometimes, it's seemingly impossible to come to an agreement. Librarians should take a deep breath and review all the options, and not be afraid to walk away. There are always alternative solutions with other vendors if the current negotiation is not proceeding to the librarian's liking.

The reality is that the information industry comprises a limited number of vendors selling to a finite number of libraries. The industry generates many billions of dollars. If the info pro has to walk away from a particular vendor, there will always be another vendor with similar products—maybe not as good as the preferred vendor's, but in reality, those other databases will work just fine 95 percent of the time. The vendor knows this and wants to keep the library's business, and will do everything possible to accomplish this goal.

In the song, "The Gambler," (written by Don Schlitz) Kenny Rogers sings: "You got to know when to hold 'em, know when to fold 'em, know when to walk away and know when to run." A rep knows that time is money and that too much time spent on people who are unreasonable and difficult to deal with will ultimately yield no return on investment. Reps need to assess each opportunity and decide how much time to invest.

KNOWLEDGE POINTS

- Selling information is a very profitable business for the vendor.

- In the negotiation, the information professional has tremendous leverage.

- For the info pro, there are four elements to a negotiation: setting objectives, setting a timetable, assembling a team, and creating a strategy.

- The objectives will change as negotiations continue. If the objectives remain stagnant, the chances of a successful conclusion are greatly diminished.

- Objections need to be addressed immediately, and if the salesperson cannot answer the question, it is not only appropriate but expected for him to say, "I don't know, and I'll get back to you with the answer."

- Both the sales rep and librarian should know when to stop negotiations. If negotiations drag on, with the parties unwilling to bend, then walking away may be the best answer.

13

Terms and Conditions

In "My Back Pages," written and sung by Bob Dylan, are the lyrics, "Yes, my guard stood hard when abstract threats too noble to neglect, Deceived me into thinking I had something to protect. Good and bad, I define these terms. Quite clear, no doubt, somehow. Ah, but I was so much older then, I'm younger than that now." I do feel that I am younger today than when I first heard this song, but reality hits when I try to win a tennis match against a person 20 years younger—most of the time the results favor the young opponent. Nevertheless, in establishing terms and conditions for a database contract, age is not a factor. The only factor is obtaining a fair agreement that makes both sides happy.

Understanding How Costs Are Set

Vendors struggle every day with the dilemma of what to effectively charge for the content they are providing. If they are an aggregator, they must take into account whatever royalty arrangements they need to pay their content providers. If they are selling original content, then the age-old question of what constitutes a fair price will be endlessly debated by the product experts, marketing group, executive council, and a virtual who's who of characters at the home office. Built into any initial cost for a renewable product is the projected yearly price increase, so that a $10,000 product with a 2.5 percent yearly increase, for example, can be modeled for the company and its financial backers to show the projected income over the next 5 to 7 years. Companies take these calculations very seriously and use them to make financial projections for their executives, owners, and financial partners. Many companies have an elaborate pricing structure that limits the salesperson to a specified discount over a specific amount of time when offering incentives to the customer. Usually sales reps can offer a given percentage off the price without manager approval. The manager then has a certain percentage he can approve, the VP has a certain percentage, and so on up the ladder. Therefore, it makes sense for the info pro to ask for a discount. It's not as easy to get one approved if the percentage requested exceeds the company's guidelines. Remember, for the company, it's all about maximizing revenue.

In actuality, salespeople don't like to give discounts because a lower price means less commission. So there is the incredible tug between the vendor and the customer as to which side can come away from the negotiating table with the best deal. The salesperson walks that fine line of serving two masters: the company and the customers. Not an easy role, but successful reps know how to do this quite well.

Consumers of any product like to believe that vendors are conducting exhaustive reviews and price modeling when deciding what to charge for their product line. But, in the end, the vendor's job is to maximize profits. That being said, in order to make a profit the vendor must have a unique product attached to superior customer service and the latest technology. It's nice to have exclusive products, but there are usually alternatives for the library to consider if a certain vendor proves difficult to deal with.

Most vendors want to sell their products to as many customers as possible, and, to do so, they must offer their products at a reasonable cost. Competition keeps vendors honest, making it absurd to sell a product either well below or above the prices charged by their competitors.

Some companies in the information industry are owned by large multinational conglomerates. In those cases, the benefit of being a subsidiary of a larger entity is that the information industry company can severely undercut the prices being charged by their competitors. While this may be good for consumers in the short run, eventually that price will have to become normalized (meaning that the discounted price will eventually rise close to the competition's price).

I am reminded of the adage "it's too good to be true." The incredible deal of today is the lousy deal of tomorrow. Many companies develop a product as a "loss leader." The product is sold at a very low price to entice customers to do business with that company. While a library may benefit today from that low price, once that company secures its business, the price will probably rise significantly in the future. This is the classic "bait and switch" technique used by unscrupulous vendors. Anything that sounds too good to be true probably isn't worth consideration.

As previously mentioned, salespeople walk a fine line between the customer and the company, which is why, when it comes to pricing issues, many companies not only consider the opinion of the VP of sales but also talk with the reps. Ultimately, questions of pricing and contract terms are usually left to a group within the company and take into account the sales team's opinion.

For the rep, the price is the price is the price—in other words, a sales rep has only so much leeway in granting a discount. The pertinent details are usually transmitted in a group conference call or a memo as illustrated here:

To: Sales staff
From: VP of Sales
Re: The new Archeological Database
    Today, we have finalized the pricing of the XYZ Archeological Ruins Database. Please contact your customers immediately since we will be able to grant

access by the first of next month. The cost will be $3,700 the first year (introductory discount) and $4,500 year two, and by the third year, we expect it to be priced at $4,750 going forward.

For every "new business" order for this exciting offering, we will add $100 to your commission. Do not add any further discounts to the prices described as I have instructed your managers not to grant a further reduction in price.

Good luck and good selling!

The sales team has its marching orders. Whether the reps feel that this price is fair or not, their job is to sell the product, end of story. The rep is judged on sales results, and, in the infinite wisdom of the folks at the home office, the price published is the price to be paid. If the sales team collectively has trouble selling the product at the published price, then another discussion will probably take place and may lead to an adjustment.

Product Use Terms and Conditions

The buying decision often turns on how liberal the vendor's terms and conditions are. For the information professional, understanding this part of the decision-making process will give you an indication of how much the vendor is willing to give away to obtain your business.

Vendors realize that by granting more liberal terms and conditions they may increase sales, but will that increased business be profitable if the discounts are too liberal? It may not be if the more liberal terms and conditions extend access to people who normally would have bought the product for themselves. For example, sales to public libraries represent a dilemma for the vendor in that there may be some people using the public library who normally would pay for the same service. Can the vendor sell enough product to enough public libraries to counteract the increased usage of that product by potential customers who are using the database for free at their local public library?

Similarly, different markets can represent increased revenue flows for the vendor. Some companies sell the majority of their products to corporate libraries. Inevitably, they look at the nonprofit, academic market as a possible alternative market. While that's a good idea, each market—corporate, academic, legal, government—comes with unique requirements. The vendor has to be prepared to make some accommodations in terms and conditions when crossing into new markets.

I once worked for a company that sold its product exclusively to banks and Fortune 500 firms. To increase revenue, I suggested that it create a subset of products aimed specifically at the higher education market. I reasoned that this could be a new source of revenue for the company, while at the same time introducing the product to future users headed into the business world.

The owner/president of the company understood intellectually that the developmental costs for creating the new product for this new market would be very low and that the chance for a significant profit quite high. We reasoned that by embargoing the content in the academic market offering by a few weeks, we would be able to differentiate that offering from the commercial one.

He liked the embargo idea, but when I proposed that we give the academic market a significant price discount, he balked. We finally settled the money issue when I agreed to lessen the amount of the discount. Everything seemed fine until we had the following conversation:

> "Mike, what if an investment banker in New York who works for a firm that we have not yet sold to has a kid in college at the University of Michigan? And this guy's son or daughter in grad school passes our information

to their father because the library on campus has the data. Can we prevent this from happening?" he asked.

"It's all in the terms and conditions," I replied. "If you want greater distribution of your content, and by that I mean making it available for university students, then yes, you run the risk of having some kid in some school pass your data off to their parents or siblings located anywhere else in the world. It's not likely, but it could conceivably happen."

"So how *do* I prevent this from happening?" he asked.

To ease his mind regarding this highly unlikely eventuality, we crafted language in the terms and conditions of the agreement that would prohibit the sharing of the company's data from the campus to non-students. The company president was relieved to know that his data was safely ensconced in the university. We created a new product with a minimum of developmental costs and produced a new revenue stream for the company.

This example illustrates a relatively quick method for a small company with very few databases for sale to increase revenues. In this case, we tightened the terms and conditions of the agreements and were able to increase revenue. On the other hand, for companies with a larger business base, allowing for more liberal contractual terms and conditions could lead to a drop in business. This is because with the easing of terms, libraries may find it easy to allow patrons to do more copying and sharing, which may result in fewer sales.

Payment Terms

The negotiating process inevitably includes payment terms. Large information providers have incredibly complex accounting departments that are well versed in what the company will and will not accept. Often these companies will be amenable to considering special payment terms to suit the customer. For the information professional, requesting special payment terms can be an integral part of the negotiation process.

As stated in previous chapters, once the first meeting is held and the library expresses an interest in a possible purchase of data, the information professional immediately gains the upper hand. The salesperson wants to sell you something and is eager to "sweeten the deal." The info pro needs to articulate what the library wants, not only in relation to the product but also with regard to other incentives that could seal the deal.

For example, if the product being considered will stretch over two fiscal year periods, would the information provider accept half of the payment upon concluding a signed agreement and the rest 6 months later? If the answer is yes, can that deal be made without interest?

How much of a discount will the company grant if the library is used as a demonstration site for the newly purchased database?

What are the percentage increases for renewal? Part of the negotiations might be to cap the renewal rate at a specific percentage. In these times of low interest rates, cost-of-living percentages could be a very attractive term for the library, especially when projecting future costs.

A well thought-out plan using the leverage gained by the library during the negotiation process could conceivably save the institution many thousands of dollars over the term of the subscription.

The rep will respond to the librarian's requests and will take those ideas back to the manager of the department. One of the reasons I strongly recommend an agenda for a substantive meeting on "t's and c's" is that it spells out everyone's topics for the meeting in advance. If, for example, the library is asking for a deep discount that the rep knows he can't approve, he will most assuredly bring along his boss who has that authority. Having the boss at the meeting allows for immediate approval of a certain discount, which means the deal gets done in less time.

KNOWLEDGE POINTS

- Selling an exclusive product is a great position for a vendor to be in. However, for most database products on the market today, there are alternative choices available (similar databases for about the same amount of money).

- Granting terms that expand access to a product helps the library, but it may ultimately cause the vendor to lose business.

- If the information professional doesn't ask pertinent questions prior to, during, and after the meeting, it is conceivable that money will be left on the table—money that could be used by the library for other resources.

14

Sales Satisfaction

In the classic Rolling Stones song, "(I Can't Get No) Satisfaction" (written by Mick Jagger and Keith Richards), Jagger sings about not getting satisfaction in his daily life. Sales satisfaction, on the other hand, can be attained provided the customer and the salesperson are able to communicate, understand, and help one another.

This chapter examines sales satisfaction, mileposts in communications, and the post-sales relationship from the perspectives of both the information professional and the sales rep. Optimally, these perspectives align, but when that is not the case, honest and open communication is the key to getting (and keeping) satisfaction.

Sales Satisfaction
For the Information Professional

As the purchaser of information products, the info pro may or may not be satisfied. Sometimes a product purchased with good intent simply does not get the expected use, has outlived its purpose, or has too many technological flaws to warrant continuation. A good salesperson continually monitors product satisfaction after the sale. But what if the rep or the vendor is not following up with you?

Information professionals should let their sales reps know how the new product is faring with their internal customers.

Maybe more training is needed. Maybe there are technical flaws that, if resolved, will make it easier to use and, therefore, more attractive. Or, maybe it is the wrong product for the organization's current needs.

It is also possible that the info pro and her library are perfectly satisfied. Whatever the case, the sales rep needs to know how everything is working. The information professional's role in sales satisfaction is to communicate with the salespeople who sold the product or whoever is the "rep du jour" and inform them as to how the product is being received at the library. The last thing the rep wants is to make the obligatory contact for renewal 90 to 120 days before the anniversary date only to find out that the product is not being used and the library is going to cancel the service:

> "We bought that new physics database that you were touting, based on initial reviews. Unfortunately, it has not lived up to expectations. We won't be renewing it," the librarian says to the rep.

This is not the kind of news that any salesperson likes to hear. Had the rep been doing his job more effectively, he would have been tracking the usage and could easily have found out that this database was not getting much use. In his defense, if the rep has a significantly large number of customers, tracking each one is not an easy task. In some bigger companies, whole departments are set up to track usage and report to the appropriate rep on their customers' use of the databases. Still, there are few excuses for the rep who doesn't know what his customers' usage patterns are.

The information professional likewise needs to carefully monitor the usage of products throughout the subscription period. Most database companies have a tracking feature that allows for instant analysis of the usage of their products. By being proactive in doing the analysis, the librarian can inform the salesperson well before the renewal anniversary if the product is not working as promised. When inadequacies of a purchased database are noted before the renewal date, the vendor can take action to address them, thus possibly avoiding a cancellation in favor of a satisfied customer.

For the Salesperson

Salespeople are urged to "close" the sale, which means obtaining the customer's approval on an order form so that the company can send out an invoice. Quite frankly, it's hard enough to close a sale, but it is infinitely more difficult to keep it closed. In the information industry, databases are sold on a subscription basis, so as information professionals know all too well, any sale made means at least a yearly visit afterward from the salesperson.

The salesperson's role between those annual visits is to make sure the customer is consistently pleased with the service being provided through regular visits, phone conversations, and/or email communications. Therefore, it is incumbent upon the salesperson to keep in touch with the customer and to find out if there are any problems so they can be tended to immediately. Lack of attention by the sales rep is the first step in losing the order at renewal time.

At one of my jobs, I worked in a major accounts role where we were required to see all our customers on a quarterly basis. Considering that many of those accounts were spending in the six figures, it was a wise methodology on the part of the company, since no one wanted to lose a large customer at renewal time. If I visited the customer on February 1, for example, I was required to schedule another appointment 90 days in the future. My usual routine, which I've mentioned earlier in this book, would go something like this. After reviewing my to-do items I would say:

> "Joanne, today's meeting was most productive and I hope I answered all your questions. I'd like to schedule our next meeting. How does May 1 look to you?"

"Mike, that's a long way in the future. I guess I'm OK with that date," was the usual reply.

"Let's make that date tentative and we can confirm as we get closer to May 1," was my response.

This was just a way for me as the sales executive to "pencil in" the next time we expected to get together. Moreover, it gave me the scheduling prompt to keep in contact with the client as May 1 approached.

Mileposts in Communication
For the Information Professional

When it comes to communication with a customer, what is considered too much and what is not enough? Everyone's tolerance for communication is different. Throughout my sales career, I have always made it a practice to keep in touch as much as the customer needs—or with some people, as much as the customer will tolerate.

The customer sets the tone for communication and therefore can set the schedule for how often she'd like to hear from each of the reps that service her account. Given the number of salespeople who will inevitably beat a path to a library's door, it is wise for info pros to set a limited schedule that they can live with. Salespeople will appreciate the ground rules, and most of them will adhere to a schedule.

Librarians need to remember it's *their* time. Although meeting with prospective customers is certainly a part of their day-to-day responsibilities, sales reps have other tasks to complete. The salesperson will appreciate knowing when to call and when not to call.

When those calls do occur, the information professional should use the time to communicate to the rep whether the product is being effectively used and to lay out any issues that need to be addressed.

For the Salesperson

For the sales rep, ongoing communication is a significant part of the job. The rep is mindful that the sale must remain closed and at the same time is looking to set the stage for the next purchase. It is therefore very important to maintain a high level of customer satisfaction, not only with the last product purchased but with all products purchased. That way when a new database is introduced, it has a better-than-average chance of being accepted by the customer. The rep will therefore schedule visits to check on the customer's satisfaction with the current suite of products and to begin introducing new products that may be of interest to the library's users.

The frequency of those visits should be mutually agreed upon by the sales rep and the information professional. These communications mileposts provide both parties with an opportunity to explore the current status and future direction of their business relationship. The rep's purpose at this stage is to make sure the customer is happy. If the customer is happy, then the current products will probably be renewed, and the possibility of additional sales is greatly enhanced.

Once again, I cannot stress enough the enormous amount of leverage the library has in the sales process. If the information professional communicates effectively, the salesperson will immediately know her boundaries for contacting him and will work within those guidelines to provide the library with the best products that the company has to offer.

In post-sales communication with the information professional, the sales rep should ask:

- Are you satisfied with the products you have purchased from us?

- Can we do better?

- Is there something else we can provide?

- Do you need any more training?

The sales rep has a vested interest in making sure the librarian is happy since this is a business with renewable products. The reps know, and their managers certainly know, that part of their responsibility is to be in regular communication with the library.

The Post-Sales Relationship

If you think the customer relationship stops once the sale has been made, think again. That's when the hard work begins, and relationships are challenged. Both the information professional and the sales organization need to work to build and maintain the post-sales relationship.

The info pro's role in keeping the sale closed is to monitor how the product is being used at the library. Here are some questions to consider:

- Is the information contained in the database current?

- Can the library patrons use the product with minimal training?

- Does it get a lot of use or is it ignored?

- Is the product ever unavailable due to crashes or other technical problems?

- Have the users provided any positive or negative feedback?

By monitoring all aspects of the product's use, the info pro can immediately tell the sales rep the good, the bad, and the ugly. This is a very important part of their relationship, and the communication benefits librarian and rep alike.

KNOWLEDGE POINTS

- Sales satisfaction can only be achieved when both the sales rep and the information professional are in communication.

- Carefully scheduled communications ensure that the time spent together is productive.

- The post-sale relationship between the parties is just as important as the relationship that led to the sale, if not more so.

Coping With Change

In the hit song "Changes," written and sung by David Bowie, he croons: "Ch-ch-ch-ch-changes (Turn and face the strain). Ch-ch-changes, Just gonna have to be a different man. Time may change me, But I can't trace time." Yup, as Bowie says, you're "just gonna have to be a different man" because changes are all around us. For any of us to survive and thrive in this ever-changing information environment, we must confront, connect to, and cope with the changes that appear in our lives. We must confidently face them head on.

Both salespeople and information professionals face an ever-changing landscape. Companies and individuals that do not recognize the new paradigms and learn to adapt will most certainly be left behind. But no one—with the exception of a wet baby—really likes change.

I began my career selling microfiche, moved on to CD-ROMs, and then to online products and ebooks. Some readers of this book may have bought or sold microfiche early in their careers. Other readers may never even have encountered it. Microfiche is simply not part of today's information environment. We all change, buyers and sellers alike, to accommodate new technologies and new methods of information delivery.

Rigid resistance to change may work for you in your personal life (although I doubt it), but if you are resistant to change in the business world, you may as well give up now and stop wasting everyone else's time. I can unequivocally say that being averse to change in business will guarantee failure.

Change Comes to Sales Organizations

More than ever before, sales organizations are facing an ever-changing environment. Customers and prospects are more 'sophisticated. Competitors are all using the same prospecting tools to ferret out new clients. If a company's customer support group is doing anything short of a phenomenal job, its customers will reach out to another provider of the same information. If a company's interaction with clients and prospects is considered merely "good," it's not good enough.

The basic reason is simple. The internet has leveled the playing field. No single company has a clear advantage over another. All company executives have the same access to the same body of information. In the past, the clever sales rep or seasoned sales manager could turn to unique sources to find the good leads. It's not as easy to find and keep the "hot leads" anymore.

The internet has changed the environment for purchasers as well, thanks to social media and the strong networking and research abilities of information professionals. Customers will find any weaknesses in a product almost instantaneously. Deliver a database with key facts missing or a seemingly obtuse interface, and you're history. Create a platform that doesn't work properly, and criticism crops up all over the internet. Fail to answer customer inquiries quickly and efficiently, and you'll hear about it from the customer, and from other customers as well, or see it written about in a blog. If a sales rep is not astute, he will quickly lose the business to a competitor. The competition is just waiting for someone to make a mistake so it can pick up the pieces of failed promises and unanswered questions, and swoop in to steal customers. Today's information marketplace is as transparent as it's ever been.

Sales trainer extraordinaire Jay Shelov often said, "Change is security and security is change." To be successful, salespeople all need to embrace the concept of change. Info pros as well need to embrace the changing environment.

How can a sales organization embrace the concept of change and use it to its advantage? First, adopt the attitude that change is good. Then resolve to work smarter and be more creative than ever before. Business as usual will not work. If a company is doing business the same way it was even 6 months ago, it is out of step.

Change Comes to Libraries

The ways in which libraries purchase materials has changed significantly over the years. What used to be a paper-based system has given way to clever software designed to make acquisitions more efficient. For example, in the January 8, 2013 issue of *Publishers Weekly*, Brian Kenney, library director of the White Plains (NY) Public Library, talks about a "purchase alert" report that tells him what items have received the largest numbers of holds—or reserves—from his customers. This gives him great insight into what titles the patrons of the library are requesting. According to Kenney, "The report immediately generates a rush order; we always buy at least one copy of a book for every four holds, sometimes for every three. After all, if 40 people in my community have bothered to reserve a book, I can safely assume another 80 or 100 want to read it."

Libraries throughout the country are using this type of report to buy materials that their patrons want. The capacity to translate patron preferences into purchase orders delights not only the people using the library but also the vendors who service the library.

Of course, the emergence of ebooks has changed the equation of how libraries buy and what they buy and in what format. In the article "4 Ways to Purchase Ebooks for Your Library" (June

13, 2012, Open Education Database), Ellyssa Kroski talks about different sources for library ebooks: aggregators, publishers, wholesalers, and consortia. The info pro needs to be aware of the various pricing schemes and be able to negotiate the best deal with the seller that offers the most cost-efficient terms.

The reality is that information professionals must be conversant in all the latest software and apps to identify trends, buy resources, and manage their libraries. More time has to be devoted to understanding the new ways of doing business.

Leadership

What are your sales leaders or your library management doing to lead staff in navigating the changing landscape? Does the staff have confidence that their leaders are in tune with the changing times? If not, their lack of confidence usually translates to a lack of performance.

Sales Leadership

Sales organizations bestow very creative titles on the men and women who direct their sales teams: Senior Vice President of Global Sales, Senior National Sales Director, Sales Manager for World Markets, Executive Sales Director of the Americas, Inter-Galactic Chief of Sales, and so on. The titles get more creative, but the job is the same no matter what it says on the business card. The top person, the top dog, the big Kahuna, or whoever is on top of the sales management pyramid should be simply "The Sales Leader." That's the title that really describes the job.

Salespeople work in an ever-changing environment. If the company's sales leaders are stagnant and don't take the lead to show the sales force how to adapt to the changes around them, it is easy to predict that the company will fall behind the competition and ultimately fail miserably. It's up to the sales leader to chart the course, set the direction, create the strategy, and spend more time in the field and less time in the office.

If the sales leaders are spending more than 50 percent of the time in the office, they are not fulfilling their responsibilities. No one has patience for armchair quarterbacks. Directing the troops from a safe place is unacceptable. A true sales leader travels with the sales force. When the top sales executive goes on a call with the sales rep, the client takes notice. It shows respect for the customer, strengthens the relationship with the client, and will probably help close the initial sale and subsequent renewal.

It boils down to this: People do *not* want to be managed, they want to be led. The sales leader is responsible for long-term planning, and that job requires a strategic thinker. Will the current products offered by the company remain suitable to be sold for the next 5 years? Can they be improved? If not, what is the sales leader doing to find suitable replacement products? What product is the company's best seller? Does the sales leader know why it is successful? How can the company produce similar products to emulate that success?

Is the sales force at peak performance? Unless sales leaders craft and implement strategies for the future, they will be mired in repetition, fall behind the competition, and will not be able to guide their sales team effectively. Have the sales leader's close advisors earned the respect of the sales team, or are they just "yes" men and women? We are judged by the company we keep. If the second-in-command does not have the support or the respect of the team, then disaster awaits.

The sales leader must actively seek out and interview prospective new candidates for the team, and must be the last word on the hiring of salespeople. Even if there are no open slots on the sales team, the sales leader should be constantly interviewing potential candidates, so that when an opening occurs there is a list of viable candidates who could immediately step in. If you want a world-class sales team, you have to go out and find them. The really good ones won't necessarily come to your door. On a related note, the sales leader needs to keep, nurture, and promote the top performers on the team (the top

20 percent) and replace the members of the group who are not at peak performance (the bottom 20 percent).

If the reps think their sales manager is behind the times and not in tune with the latest technologies, or not listening to new suggestions from the field, the smart ones will ultimately look for a job elsewhere, somewhere with a more enlightened management team. When the reps are spending valuable time looking for a new job, products will go unsold, customers will not be contacted, and prospects won't be seen. And that means quotas will not be reached. The ripple effect of out-of-touch management on the bottom line will be felt throughout the company, up through senior management and, ultimately, the ownership.

A salesperson needs to make it easier for the customer to buy the company's products. The approval process for buying a product today, whether by a library, corporation, or government agency, is taking longer than ever before. Budgets are reduced and closely scrutinized; more people are involved during the approval process. While a few years ago it took 30 to 60 days to finalize an order, it now takes 90 to 120 days for the signed paperwork to be approved, booked, and invoiced.

Customer Support, Order Fulfillment, or whatever you call the group that processes the sales paperwork for your organization needs to streamline the process:

- Allow the customer to authorize less paperwork

- Make it as easy as possible to buy products

- Reduce the number of pages on order authorization forms

- Have lawyer(s) on staff to respond immediately to potential customers' legal questions

Lengthy order forms awash in legalese are an invitation for the customer's lawyer to take a significant amount of time to review the forms and show his organization that vendors can't bamboozle the company. It's highly unlikely that any lawyer whose job it is to review a sales contract will conveniently send back his comments to coincide with the sales rep's time schedule. Therefore, the easier it is for a lawyer to approve the contract, the faster a vendor can expect acceptance.

In short, there is a profound difference between *management* and *leadership*. Management produces orderly results and has a role to play in recordkeeping, budgets, and tracking the progress of sales activities. Leadership is something vastly different. Leadership sets the direction for change and implements it. Successful salespeople want to learn from their sales leaders.

Leadership in the Library

Much like sales leaders, library directors must embrace their leadership role. Because like the sales team, the library staff needs leaders they can follow and trust in these changing times.

Dr. Jeff Weddle of the University of Alabama School of Library and Information Studies suggests that a library director must wear many hats, including "visionary leadership, institutional value setter, mentor, bearer, and exerciser of authority and responsibility for the library and focus on serving the needs of library users" (bama.ua.edu/~jweddle/Week9and10.ppt). In this one sweeping statement, Dr. Weddle sums up what the library director of today must do to be successful in all facets of the library's operations.

Hiring is another key responsibility of the library director. Throughout my sales career, I had the pleasure of working with and knowing Paula Kaufman, most recently the dean of libraries and university librarian at the University of Illinois. In one of our many conversations, we touched on how she manages such a large and diverse staff at her institution. She said that the key was to hire competent people that she trusted and let them do their jobs.

Much like a business, a library needs to satisfy its current customers and attract new ones as well. How does the library make itself more attractive so as to get more people to use the resources provided? Marketing the library's resources is often a good way to solidify and improve attendance, and library leaders should make this one of their priorities. Many vendors provide libraries with glossy handouts describing the many strong points of the databases currently being provided to the library. Using the vendor to help publicize the library's holdings is a great way to increase library usage.

Speaking of vendors, if a library does significant business with a particular vendor, the library director should be aware of how many times a senior sales executive from that company has visited the library within the last 12 months. If those meetings have been few or nonexistent, the director should question how much the vendor values the library's business. Sales leaders should be consistently meeting with library staff to understand what is most relevant for library patrons. The library director should establish a direct line to the senior management of the vendor if possible.

Reinventing Yourself

Anyone who has been in the business world for more than 10 years knows that the road to success is a rough one. It's filled with potholes, bumps, dangerous curves, and detour signs. In his book *The Winner Within: A Life Plan for Team Players* (Berkeley Trade, 1994), world-class basketball coach and motivational speaker Pat Riley refers to those bumps in the road as unexpected thunderbolts from the sky. Riley points out that we all have to cope with those inevitable changes that life throws at us. Those thunderbolts usually appear without warning and always at the worst possible times in our lives.

Executives in all lines of work who have successfully coped with "thunderbolts" of change will tell you they have "reinvented" themselves many times in their career. You cannot grow; you cannot succeed unless you reinvent yourself. In any business or any library, reinvention is not a luxury, it's a necessity. I have reinvented myself many times over the years. I may not always have liked the prospect, and, yes, it was uncomfortable at times, but I can say from personal experience that reinvention works. If you're looking forward to a long career as a salesperson or as an information professional, be prepared for reinvention.

In my first sales job I eventually rose from sales rep to VP. Along the way, in my 20-year tenure, that company was bought and sold five times. The resulting changes required repeated reinvention, but that process allowed me to survive and thrive. Every time I got comfortable with the latest ownership team, new owners came in with their own preferred management team and style. Oh, I would realize, it's reinvention time again. I can assure you that "Reinvention Time" is not as pleasant as "Miller Time," but to enjoy many more Miller Times you have to first work on your "Reinvention Time" skills.

When management changes, everything that you have previously accomplished, everything you thought you knew, everything that made you comfortable will be questioned and challenged. If you've been through this, you know that new ownership can mean proving yourself all over again.

I always had a survival mentality—I was not going to let anyone minimize the work that I had previously done or let them forget the accomplishments that were the cornerstone of my successes. With that in mind, I took on all the new challenges placed in my path. However, as I noted in Chapter 5, everyone is listening to the same radio station: W.I.I.F.M. New management wanted to know what this guy named Mike could do for them. It didn't matter what I had accomplished in the past. It was, What can this guy do for us today? and if he succeeds, maybe tomorrow?

In reinventing myself, I took tried and true skills learned in the past and applied them to a new team of managers. I was thereby able to show them that I could work in their stadium under their rules.

For the sales staff, reinvention and embracing change are vital for success. They can't fight change. It's there every day in the form of new technologies, new management, new organizational direction, and different territories. Information professionals are also undergoing constant reinvention. They, too, are encountering new management, mergers, new mandates, and updated technologies. This not an evolution, this is a revolution.

KNOWLEDGE POINTS

- Change is all around us. We need to embrace change, not fight it.

- Sales leaders create strategies, set the vision, and travel with the sales force.

- Library directors should focus on the needs of the library's constituents and recognize the need to market the library's resources.

- We need to constantly reinvent ourselves to keep up with the ever-changing information landscape.

Epilogue

"Should I stay or should I go?" is a line from the song by the same name by The Clash from their classic *Combat Rock* album. It describes the dilemma of virtually all employees deciding their future at their respective jobs.

A former business colleague recently called, someone I had worked with for a number of years. Although we often did not see eye-to-eye on business issues, we developed a mutual respect that turned into a solid professional friendship.

He told me that after 16 years of working for the same company, he had decided to give his 2 weeks notice. He is a well-respected and talented person, but he decided to leave the company because the situation there had become intolerable for him. He felt that he was becoming stagnant.

This is a case of a company failing to recognize and retain a productive and knowledgeable employee. The company will inevitably hire someone else. That new person may eventually be better or worse than my colleague who left, but meanwhile there will be a period of time for training and ramp-up with no guarantee of success for that new hire. In the end, the company suffers. It has lost an experienced person who not only knows the job well after 16 years but also knows the "ins and outs" of the culture of the company, something that can't be taught in a short period of time.

The employee, on the other hand, usually comes out ahead by leaving for greener pastures. If that person is talented and has significant industry experience, another job is most definitely in the wings. So what initially looks like a difficult decision for the employee becomes a positive career move.

After that phone call, I thought of a point in my own career when I made a similar decision. My first sales job at Disclosure lasted 20 years. I literally grew up there. I started as a sales rep and eventually became the VP of sales. After many years and several different owners, I sadly realized that this company was no longer a good fit for me. It was a chore to get up each day and go to work.

On a fateful day (for me, at least), I met with the president of the company and resigned. As I left the office, I gave a huge sigh of relief. All the tension that had built up over the last, awful year magically evaporated into the afternoon air. Of course, that tension returned a bit later when I realized that I now needed to find a job. But subsequently I did find one, and after that another one, and then another, all leading to an even more successful 14 years, replete with world travel, meeting new people, and successful sales results. During those next 15 years, I used the skills gained from the first 20 to continue to grow. Most of all, I added to my maturity as a sales leader.

Reading the signposts of a career path is an essential component of anyone's growth and success. Too many people fail to see the writing on the wall and remain stuck in unhealthy work (or personal) situations. If you're unhappy at work and that unhappiness has continued for a long period of time, you will not be a very pleasant person, either at work or, most probably, at home.

Assessing Your Career

Constant assessment of your career is essential. Are you content with the current management? Is there a path to career advancement? Are you happy with your current responsibilities? Can you see yourself staying here for another 5, 10, or 15 years? If any of these questions elicits a negative response, you need not only to read the signposts but also to act on what they are saying to you. It's time to investigate another employment path.

In every situation, personal or business, when confronted with a dilemma, you only have three basic choices. You can either:

1. Accept the situation

2. Reject the situation

3. Try to change it

There is one piece of advice that has stayed with me all these years, one that I have followed religiously: Always have fun and make money wherever you work.

My first boss continually reminded me, "Mike, if either of these two elements is missing from your job, you need to seriously consider making a change." I have taken that advice seriously and used it many times to my benefit. Life is too short for you to be continually upset at work. Showing up at a job where there is no appreciation or possibility of advancement can only lead to aggravation.

Management usually takes the narrow view that money is the most important factor for employees. This is not true. Studies that measure what employees want from their jobs usually show that higher compensation comes in at number three or four on the list.

The number one motivation for employees is the desire to make a contribution toward the betterment of their organization. People want to feel that they are important to the organization's growth and well-being. They want to believe that their ideas are being considered by management.

When management rejects your input, it's time to read the signposts. When management tells you that you will have the same job for the next 10 years with no chance of advancement, it's time to read the signposts. When you don't want to get out of bed in the morning and go to work, it's time to read the signposts.

How I Read a Significant Signpost of My Career

Signs are everywhere—you just have to look up and read them. There are signs that tell you where to park, when to stop, where to eat, and what's being shown at your local movie theater. These are obvious signs, part of our everyday existence. Sometimes we are not paying attention—the friendly police officer reminds you that you may not have seen the one way sign. The officer issues you a ticket so you'll remember to look more carefully from now on. The signs I'm talking about that can help you further your career may not be so obvious. But look around, and the signs are there if you care to read them.

When I began my first sales job selling subscriptions to financial information on public companies, my assigned territory was the Northeast. In addition, I was assigned clients in Manhattan from letter L through Z. That meant I could call on any financial institution in the Northeast, but in New York City my options were limited. I could call on UBS but not Goldman Sachs. I could call on Fidelity Investments in Boston, but not Fidelity in Manhattan. It was a bit confusing to me, but since I was new and inexperienced, I called on the prospects and customers delineated in the territory assigned to me.

Being eager to please, and realizing that there were very few prospects in Manhattan with names beginning with X, Y and Z— and since Maine, Vermont, and New Hampshire were not exactly hotbeds of financial activity—I spent a considerable amount of time going to Boston. Eventually, my territory was expanded to include Mid-Atlantic states. I still had the limited alphabet in New York City, but now I had many more states to visit.

Month after month, I dutifully made the appointments, got on planes, rented cars, and stayed in a variety of nondescript hotels. More often than not, I discovered that every financial institution I called on either was not interested or had already bought the service. It was very depressing.

I vividly remember one cold and rainy afternoon in the early 1980s in one of the cities in my territory. I was on my way home after a fruitless 3-day trip filled with rejection when I decided to get out of the rain before going to the airport.

I ducked into the public library, and there in front of me was an endless row of file drawers under a sign that said something along the lines of "Corporate Annual Reports." I counted 96 file drawers and went to inspect their contents.

Opening the top file drawer, I found the first company file beginning with the letter A. The file contained the annual report for American Something or Other Corporation from 1972; half of the 1973 report was missing, there was nothing for 1974, and the 1975 one had been defaced, with an eye patch and mustache drawn on the picture of the chairman on the opening page.

I continued my investigation, and it became painfully obvious that this collection was anything but complete. I even found a half-eaten French fry in one of the folders. I knew that I could sell this library a complete collection of *all* the annual reports we offered on microfiche for a reasonable cost. By buying my product, the library could free up an incredible amount of space and be assured a complete collection, now and in the future. If ever there was a win–win, this I thought was it.

I confidently went over to the librarian, announced the company I was representing, and made it clear that my product could help the library's business patrons. When the librarian initially rejected my premise, I escorted him over to the file drawers. Much to his chagrin, he had to agree that the collection was in shambles. When I pointed out the half-eaten French fry, that sealed the deal. We settled on a price for a subscription that included not only the main branch of the library but also another set of the same collection for a satellite business branch. I was assured an order would be on my desk in a few days.

I was feeling pretty good about myself as I boarded the plane to go home. My glee turned to dismay when I realized that the public library I just convinced to buy our product was not in my territory.

The next day, the following conversation took place between my and my boss:

> "Hey Steve, do we sell our products to public libraries and universities?" I asked.
>
> "We have some of those customers, but those orders came in through the mail, and no rep has ever really called on public libraries and universities," he answered.
>
> "I was in the office last week when that order from Yale University came in. Who sold that?" I inquired.
>
> "It showed up in the mail just like those other public library and university orders, and since there was no rep on the account, no commission was paid," he said wistfully.

Knowing how much revenue the Yale order had generated, and knowing how much my expected new public library order was going to be, I seized on the moment and asked, "Would you be willing to make me the university and public library specialist for the company?"

Steve laughed and asked me if I was sure I really wanted this role. If I was serious, he would think about it. I answered in the affirmative and gave him a dozen reasons why we shouldn't disregard this market, which in my opinion needed a full-time salesperson to manage it.

Early the next week, I was appointed the university and public library specialist for the company, covering the entire eastern half of the U.S. In other words, I had sales responsibility for all the universities, colleges, and public libraries east of the Mississippi River. The public library order that I had stumbled upon came in a few days after my appointment. I was laughingly accused of "sandbagging," a term I had never heard before, over a celebratory lunch at an expensive restaurant in Manhattan.

Reading the Writing on the Wall

Reading the writing on the wall, noticing the signposts on the road, reading the tea leaves, whatever you call it—it's crucial for your success. Try to understand the needs of the organization and stay attuned to management's strategic direction. That direction changes all the time, so you need to figure out how you can contribute to the achievement of their goals and yours. How can *you* make a difference?

In the example from my own career, I realized that the public sector could be a valuable market for the company. I also knew that none of the salespeople I worked with had any desire to enter that market. Those guys, including my boss, all preferred to call on J.P. Morgan as opposed to Idaho State U. They preferred to make sales calls in L.A. and Chicago as opposed to Cheyenne, Wyoming, or Lubbock, Texas. Maybe Wall Street had more panache and was more glamorous than academia, but in the end, my reading of the tea leaves brought me financial and professional success.

Being creative in the way you think about your job is critical to ensuring success. I always imagined my territory as my business. If I were the owner of this business, providing products and services to the universities and public libraries, how would I run it? Would I take that trip to the Southeast because it made good business sense, or was my real reason for going not entirely based on selling products? Am I taking the least expensive transportation that doesn't involve prolonged discomfort? Can I stay at a hotel that is comfortable but not incredibly expensive? But most of all, will the expected sales from the trip equal or exceed the cost of the journey? That was my yardstick on whether or not to make the trip. It comes down to being responsible, to myself as well as to the company.

There is a difference between being responsible and having a responsibility. My responsibility to the company was to give it 100 percent of my efforts every day in representing its products. Its responsibility to me was to provide world-class products along with world-class support for the customers and a fair compensation package.

But being responsible means going a step beyond. Here is an example to illustrate the difference. When you are walking down the corridors of your organization and you see a piece of paper on the floor, what do you do? It's not your responsibility to pick it up, but you are acting as a responsible person if you do.

The signpost I read on that cold and wet afternoon showed me an opportunity. I was having a difficult time selling the product to financial markets in the Northeast and Mid-Atlantic states, so I knew that I needed to find an alternative territory to further my career and achieve financial success. Yes, it was a risky move, and my boss had every reason to turn down my offer. But I also knew that the company was supportive of new ideas from its employees. When your company encourages fresh ideas and recognizes that those ideas are the very cornerstone of everyone's success, then you know you are working at the right place. I was blessed at that time to have a great boss and great owners in Bob Snyder and Phil Hixon.

Some 28 years later I went back to work for Bob Snyder, this time at Cambridge Scientific Abstracts, where he is now chairman of the Cambridge Information Group. I thanked him for all the years of support he had given me both at Disclosure and at Cambridge. I went on to say that he and his business partner had been instrumental in my success and that I was eternally grateful. Bob looked at me and said:

> "Mike, all we ever did for you was to give you the opportunity to fail. Luckily for all of us, you usually succeeded."

For my final knowledge point I return to what my boss Steve Goldspiel told me years ago: Have fun and make money. Make sure both of those elements are part of your job. If one of them is missing, consider leaving. If both are missing, bail out as quickly as possible.

About the Author

Photo by Scott Maynard

The name **Mike Gruenberg** is synonymous in the information services industry with winning results—in sales team development and leadership, in performance and customer satisfaction, and in selling complex information services to demanding markets worldwide. Mike's track record of more than 30 years in the industry is headlined by significant profit performance in every position he has held. Many of the salespeople he has managed and mentored have gone on to highly successful careers.

Mike is currently the president of Gruenberg Consulting, LLC (www.gruenbergconsulting.com), a firm he founded in January 2012, devoted to providing information services companies with sales source analysis, market research, executive coaching, and trade show analysis. Moreover, he has developed a program to provide best practices advice for improving negotiation skills for information professionals.

Mike lives in North Bethesda, Maryland, with his wife Barbara. He is an avid lifelong collector of music recordings and, since 2000, a columnist for an online site devoted to the latest musical trends.

Index

More Great Books from Information Today, Inc.

The Librarian's Guide to Negotiation
Winning Strategies for the Digital Age

By Beth Ashmore, Jill E. Grogg, and Jeff Weddle

Librarians negotiate every day with vendors, funding agencies, administrators, employees, co-workers, and patrons—yet the art of negotiation receives little attention in library education and training. This practical guide by three experienced librarian-negotiators will help you develop the mindset, skills, and confidence you need to negotiate effectively in any situation. The authors provide an in-depth look at negotiation in theory and practice, share tactics and strategies of top negotiators, offer techniques for overcoming emotional responses to conflict, recall successful outcomes and deals gone awry, and demonstrate the importance of negotiating expertise to libraries and library careers. The result is an eye-opening survey into the true nature of negotiation—both as a form of communication and as a tool you can use to create sustainable collections and improve library service in the digital age.

272 pp/softbound/ISBN 978-1-57387-428-1 $49.50

21 Days to Success Through Networking
The Life and Times of Gnik Rowten

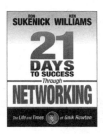

By Ron Sukenick and Ken Williams

21 Days to Success Through Networking presents a range of real-world situations, events, insights, and challenges through the eyes of a fictional character with whom almost anyone can relate. Gnik Rowten (that's "networking" spelled backward) has made a fresh start in a new city where he has few if any friends, prospects, or business contacts. Follow Gnik's life over a 3-week period as, each day, he discovers and learns tools, techniques, and strategies for effective business networking. By following Gnik's adventures and sharing his "Aha!" moments, you'll learn to extend, deepen, and effectively utilize your own personal and business networks in just 21 days.

176 pp/softbound/ISBN 978-1-937290-03-0 $15.95

Face2Face

Using Facebook, Twitter, and Other Social Media Tools to Create Great Customer Connections

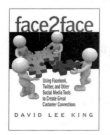

By David Lee King

With *Face2Face*, David Lee King (*Designing the Digital Experience*) presents a practical guide for any organization that aspires to create deep, direct, and rewarding relationships with patrons and prospects. King demonstrates how a range of Web 2.0 tools and techniques can be used to start and sustain conversations and humanize the organization in the eyes of those it seeks to serve. He uses real-world examples to illustrate the do's and don'ts of responding to criticism, and explains why and how listening, tone, human-centered site design, and measuring results are all critical components of any customer engagement strategy.

216 pp/softbound/ISBN 978-0-910965-99-6 $24.95

The Cybrarian's Web

An A–Z Guide to 101 Free Web 2.0 Tools and Other Resources

By Cheryl Ann Peltier-Davis
Foreword by Stephen Abram

Here is a remarkable field guide to the best of free Web 2.0 tools and their practical applications in libraries and information centers. Designed for info pros who want to use the latest tech tools to connect, collaborate, and create, you'll find resources to help you build a customized social network, start an ebook lending program, survey the library community, and more. You'll discover dozens of lesser-known resources and learn exciting new ways to use many of the most popular sites and tools. With all this and a supporting webpage, *The Cybrarian's Web* is a winner!

512 pp/softbound/ISBN 978-1-57387-427-4 $49.50